PURE
UNADULTERATED
GUTS

INSIGHTS FOR BRAVERY,
COURAGE, AND VULNERABILITY

RILEY JENSEN

Quantity sales and special discounts are available on quantity purchases by corporations, associations, and others. For details, contact the publisher at the address above.

Orders by U.S. trade bookstores and wholesalers. Email info@BeyondPublishing.net

The Beyond Publishing Speakers Bureau can bring authors to your live event. For more information or to book an event contact the Beyond Publishing Speakers Bureau speak@BeyondPublishing.net

The Author can be reached directly at BeyondPublishing.net

Manufactured and printed in the United States of America distributed globally by BeyondPublishing.net

BEYOND
PUBLISHING

New York | Los Angeles | London | Sydney

ISBN Hardcover: 978-1-63792-632-1
ISBN Softcover: 978-1-63792-633-8

To my family. Georgann, Alexis,

Jack, Karissa, KC, Crosby, Mom, and Dad.

Thank you for being my "why." Your support means

everything to me. Your belief in me continues to inspire.

TABLE OF CONTENTS

"Low self-confidence isn't a life sentence. Self-confidence can be learned, practiced, and mastered—just like any other skill. Once you master it, everything in your life will change for the better."
—Barrie Davenport[1]

1   (Davenport, 2022)

INTRODUCTION

Sports will break your heart. It's true, whether you are the best player or the worst. Somewhere, at some point in your career, your favorite sport will hurt you, challenge you, and make you struggle. You will be confronted with a myriad of mental obstacles, and you will wonder if you should even be doing this thing you love at all.

Yet, even knowing this, sports and many other things that challenge us to our core, are still worth pursuing. Pushing our boundaries to become more will always be worth it. Struggle cultivates growth, and you cannot become better without it.

The key is to be mentally prepared for when these challenges hit you head on and make you doubt everything you've done to this point. You can't afford to let these things slow you down and foster self-doubt. Because self-doubt is a tricky monster. It leads to lack of confidence, and hesitation in gameplay, causing you to lose crucial matches you could have won with a healthier mindset. This sport anxiety then continues in a vicious cycle, as each poor performance further erodes your confidence and exacerbates the problem. In extreme cases, athletes may even develop a "yips" condition, where their anxiety becomes so intense that it impairs their ability to perform even the most basic tasks.

Countless athletes around the globe struggle internally with negative self-talk, sport anxiety, fear of failure, perfectionism, embarrassment, and the overwhelming concern of letting others down. These can hold them back from achieving greatness. All of these insecurities are common, but what isn't common is seeking help to overcome them. Too often athletes struggle and fight against their own mind. They don't realize that just as they have a coach for their physical game, they could benefit from a coach for their mental game. I've experienced this emotional rollercoaster firsthand.

For as long as I can remember, I had a ball in my hands. Whether I hit a tennis ball against an unfinished wall in my parents' basement, pitched to my Dad in the front yard, or threw a Nerf football through a hoop between plastic goal posts, sports were a huge part of my childhood. As a young boy, and even now, I am fascinated with a ball. Curve balls, knuckle balls, sliders, slip pitches, fast balls, heavy throws, the deep ball, "go deep," spinning it, spirals, and arch were quickly added to my vocabulary as a young boy. I couldn't get enough, and I still can't. The repetitive nature of throwing a ball or hitting a ball better than the previous time thrilled me. And it still does to this day. After hundreds of thousands of throws, hits, serves, and catches, I still can't wait to throw the ball around with a friend at a summer BBQ or play catch with my kids on a hot summer night.

It was because of this passion that I never stopped pursuing sports. I loved that sports were essentially an act of passion dedicated to the pursuit of continuous improvement. I chased that feeling until I became the starting quarterback at Utah State University. But, I was forced to hang up my cleats when I was hit with a knockout blow in a college football game my senior year. That was the moment sports broke my heart.

Sometime in your life, somehow, some way, sports will break your heart too. It doesn't matter if you get cut from the 9th grade basketball team, if you never put on a football helmet again after your senior year in high school, or if you get benched your senior year of collegiate athletics. Your mettle will be tested, and you will have to analyze the very reasons you loved your sport to begin with.

As you can imagine, being taken out of the game completely was a blow to my identity and the plans I had for life, but the fire inside me didn't die. For a few years, I coached college football at Snow College and North Carolina State University. When that didn't fulfill my passion, I picked myself up, dusted myself off, and found myself a career in sales. For twelve years I sold. I sold radio time for the Utah Jazz. I sold hospital beds and stretchers for a company named Stryker. I also was an offensive coordinator for three local high schools. But I didn't really feel like I was chasing my dream.

Then one day, a good friend of mine said, "When are you going to quit your job and do what you were born to do? You need to be in sport psychology." I turned his words over in my mind until my wife questioned me one night after work. A hand on my arm, she said, "What are you doing? I can tell by the look on your face that you're not happy."

My friend, my wife, and everyone else who loved me were right: it was time to pursue my dream. With my wife's strong urging, it was then I took the plunge, bet on myself, and started a degree in sport psychology. And little by little, just like when I was learning to play ball—by showing up every day, loving what I do, and being excited about developing myself—I cultivated a talent for understanding the mental side of sports. As I learned, I quickly realized an athlete's mental fortitude is what separates the good from the great. I dedicated myself to helping others take their next step into greatness.

As my career advanced, I created RJ Performance Group in 2017, a sport psychology practice committed to helping athletes reach their full performance potential. Since then, I've spent years helping athletes and teams from all walks of life, including professional and Olympic athletes, overcome their psychological hurdles. I've seen the power of sport psychology in action, and after years of dedication to this practice, I decided to detail these strategies in this book. Please note that the stories in this book are used with permission of the athletes. I take pride in providing a trusting and safe place for the athletes I work with. Their names have been included to personify some of the stories and processes discussed in this book.

Within these pages, you'll find a comprehensive guide designed to help you conquer the mental challenges that have been holding you back. You'll learn how to silence the negative voices in your head and channel your anxiety into a source of motivation, confidence, and commitment. Here, we will let go of perfectionist tendencies and reduce self-talk. Sadly, studies indicate that 77% of our self-talk is negative or counterproductive. More than half! We think to ourselves, "I'm not good enough." "I don't have the connections." "Maybe they are right." "My coach didn't do enough to get me recruited." There are a million clever little lies that seep into our mind when we fail or struggle with something.

How are these thoughts working for you? Are these negative thoughts helping you succeed or helping you fail?

My guess is that most of the time you can throw these thoughts out and be better for it. Then you can dust yourself off and get back to work. You have dreams to chase. You have goals to pursue. But to do so, you need to cultivate a deep-rooted belief in yourself. With the knowledge packed within these pages, you'll learn how to build unshakeable confidence in yourself. There will be hundreds if not thousands of failures along the way—I can't make it so you won't experience failure. But I can help you fail forward and refocus yourself so you can move through life with pure unadulterated guts.

PART 1

MENTALITY IS EVERYTHING

Several years ago, I was on my way home from a party, and I was *livid*.

There were many people at this party I cared about. People who I wanted to see my best self. But, at one point, a friend of mine, probably the smartest guy in the room, if not the most clever, said, "What does Riley know? He's just a dumb jock."

Though his words were meant as a joke, on the ride home I boiled in anger. A good friend sat beside me and listened to me rant. "Why would he talk to me like that? I would never say anything like that to anyone, period!" I was pistol hot. Hotter than a snake's belly in Death Valley. "Who does this guy think he is? I promise you I am every bit as smart as that guy, I could run circles around him! That Jack Wagon is just *unkind*."

After I got done with my rant, I looked at my good friend, waiting for him to reply. Maybe even share in my anger and back me up. But, he simply looked back at me.

"Don't you have anything to say?" I said in a huff. "Or do you agree with him?"

I had laid down the line. In fact, I'd probably crossed a few by making him choose between us. But with some of the kindest eyes I had ever seen, he asked, "Are you open to some feedback?"

He didn't try to defend our common friend. Nor did he side with me. He simply asked me this question. "Do you think, maybe, how you talk about yourself to others might allow them to think they can talk about you in the same way?"

I scoffed. "What are you talking about?"

"You say you would never say anything like that about anyone, but you say it about yourself all the time. Is it possible that sometimes your self-deprecating humor gives others permission to say you're a dumb jock?"

He was right. In the name of being funny, being humble, or being easygoing, I frequently used self-deprecation as a tool against myself. I had played the "dumb jock" role plenty of times when I thought it was funny and when it served my purposes. In that moment, I realized just how important my mentality was. How I thought of myself not only shaped my own thoughts and experiences, but had shaped the way others thought about me as well. That day, I adjusted my mental attitude towards myself, and I want to help you do the same.

When self-deprecating thoughts and words become the norm, they have a negative impact on our mental state. Constantly putting ourselves down leads to feelings of low self-worth, insecurity, and self-doubt, which can ultimately hinder our ability to perform at our best. The good news is that it's possible to cultivate a positive and powerful mentality that can help you succeed in sports and in life. In the coming chapters, we will discuss how to cultivate vision, enhance your mental strength, and become gritty. These skills will help you perform at your best, even in the face of difficulty. With the right mentality, you can achieve anything you set your mind to, both on and off the field. Laird Hamilton phrased it best when he said, , "Make sure your worst enemy doesn't live between your own two ears."[1]

---

1   (Hamilton, 2023)

CHAPTER 1

CULTIVATE VISION

According to Thomas Edison, "Vision without execution is hallucination."[1] And I agree.

Vision is a way to understand your "why" in life. When you know your "why," the "what" and the "how" are easier to figure out. It's like the rudder to your ship. Without it, you are simply drifting without direction.

In my experience working with a range of individuals—from Olympic athletes to professional rodeo athletes, professional baseball players, elite archery athletes, college and professional football players, college and professional basketball players, college and high school coaches, high school athletes, and even nine-year-old soccer players—I've observed a common struggle: lack of vision.

It was George Eliot who is attributed as saying, "It's never too late to be what you ought to have been."[2] And I took those words to heart when I took an unexpected detour in life, went back to school, and faced the repercussions of going against the grain. Despite my

---

1   (Edison, n.d.)

2   (Eliot, n.d.)

apprehension and doubt from others, I refused to retreat. Why? Because I wanted to demonstrate to my children that they could achieve anything at any age, that chasing a dream isn't convenient, and the more audacious the dream, the greater the resistance—but, with a solid vision in place and hard work even in the face of resistance, they could achieve their dreams.

My intent in sharing this isn't to inflate my ego, but to illustrate. I made a drastic career change at 40, faced my fears, and several years later, I'm relishing it. The hard-earned tools and lessons from this journey are precious treasures that I use daily in my personal life and career. And stories like mine are not unique, but they do have one thing in common.

Vision.

Take the example of a man who transformed his fortunes at the age of 65 with nothing but a chicken recipe to his name. Colonel Harland Sanders offered the recipe for free to several businesses, asking only for a small percentage of sales in return. Although it sounded like a good deal, he faced rejection time and time again. Despite hearing "no" several hundred times, he refused to give up, believing his chicken recipe was genuinely special. It took a staggering 1,009 rejections before he finally received his first "yes." And that single success transformed the way Americans eat chicken today because Colonel Harland Sanders went on to create the renowned restaurant Kentucky Fried Chicken.

You don't need permission to be great. But you do need a clear vision which serves as a guiding light on your path.

Eat Your Elephant

When you chase your dreams, the big goals can be overwhelming.

I have immense goals for myself. And occasionally, the loftiness of my goals are debilitating. But I know I don't have to feel this way. The secret is to break these goals down into smaller, more manageable tasks.

Researchers at Harvard and the University of Southern California found offering small, even meaningless rewards can increase motivation. These token rewards, however arbitrary, inspire people to keep working towards a larger goal. By structuring small doses of dopamine throughout the day, we can perform better and longer, even if the tasks are menial. And you can use daily, small, and well-planned goals to work towards the big ones, giving yourself a reward along the way. Just like with dogs and dolphins, a small "reward" for a job or a task completed can make all the difference.

Alabama Coach Nick Saban is known for using a tactic like this. Instead of advising his players to think about the championships or winning the game, he urges them to focus only on the current play, which typically lasts seven seconds. He says, "Don't think about winning the SEC Championship. Don't think about the national championship. Think about what you need to do in this drill, on this play, in this moment." Coach Saban has won six national championships in the last thirteen years. Seems like this tactic works well for him and his players!

That's the process: Think about what we can do today, in this moment, to reach our goals.

"How do you eat an elephant? One bite at a time." Even the most formidable tasks can be tackled by breaking them down into manageable steps. This may sound simple, and it is, but simple is not always easy. However, doing something simple, and doing it well can lead to huge results. As an individual, no matter your position, the single most important thing you can do is simplify the job. The creation of micro goals each day can help you to release healthy amounts of dopamine into your system on a consistent basis so you can keep grinding toward your long-term goal.

Celebrate The Moment

Dan and Chip Health wrote a fantastic book called "The Power of Moments." And in it, they talk fervently about the ability to recognize a moment and how to celebrate it correctly.

For example, we have five, ten, twenty-five, and even fifty year anniversaries to celebrate our marriage, but do we ever celebrate how many books we've read? We celebrate graduation from school, but do we celebrate the number of miles we have walked or run in our lifetime?

The more moments you celebrate, the more motivated you'll feel to keep going. And that internal fire starts first thing in the morning. Begin by winning the morning with three non-negotiable tasks to set the tone for the rest of your day. When you start your day on a triumphant note, you'll feel more confident and in control, giving you a "you've got this" mindset. Keep in mind these non-negotiable tasks should be intentional and not simply part of your daily autopilot routine, like taking a shower, brushing your teeth, or eating breakfast.

Instead, consider more deliberate actions, such as dedicating time to reading a thought-provoking book, prayer and scripture reading, whipping up a nutritious protein shake, taking a cold shower, or setting aside a few moments for mindfulness or meditation. By incorporating these intentional tasks into your morning routine, you'll be primed for success and ready to take on whatever the day has in store.

You can make it easier on yourself to remember these non-negotiables by using the concept of habit stacking, introduced by James Clear, in his book "Atomic Habits." It involves connecting an activity or goal to a time period when you're already productive (like in the morning when you get ready for the day) because it can be more difficult to remember what your three non-negotiables were at 3pm. In other words, you have a better chance of completing new and important tasks by hitching them to a time period during the day in which tasks are already being accomplished.

This approach makes it easier to establish habits by leveraging your existing productive routines, and gives you early wins you can celebrate!

Imagery

Imagery, an essential tool in sport psychology, goes beyond visualization.

When using visualization, one typically imagines themselves achieving a particular objective (such as winning a race) to reinforce a desired outcome. Imagery, however, is the mental process of creating or experiencing sensory impressions in one's mind using visual, auditory, olfactory, and tactile sensations. It goes beyond envisioning success to actually living it.

Science Behind Imagery

Through imagery, you can convince your body (and your muscle) that you have actually practiced and gained the same benefits as if you had actually moved your body.

There is a fatty substance in our brain called the myelin sheath, which was discovered while researching a cure for multiple sclerosis (MS). This sheath, similar to insulation on electrical cables, prevents energy loss from the brain's electrical signals. Researchers observed the myelin sheath and found when we activate neural pathways repeatedly, such as practicing the perfect shot or catch, our brain wraps these pathways with a layer of insulation, which allows the pathways to fire more efficiently and with greater focus. Before this was discovered, many coaches and professionals referred to the skill gained from repetition as "muscle memory." But now we know, when you practice something repeatedly, you are actually building myelin sheath around your neural pathways, making them more accessible.

For example, Einstein's neural pathways likely had more myelin sheath wrapped around the areas related to math and science in his brain. Similarly, an athlete would have more myelin sheath around neural pathways focused on enhanced coordination and movement. This is why people have fallen in love with the 10,000-hour rule—it represents the time it takes to create a substantial amount of myelin sheath around specific pathways, which leads to increased proficiency in a particular skill or subject.

Now, here's where the cool part comes in. When you walk through an imagery session using all five senses, your body doesn't know the difference between imagery and reality! Meaning a good imagery session will build myelin sheath along your neuro pathways just like an actual practice session would.

In a Ted talk on how to practice effectively, Annie Bosler and Don Greene discussed a study where 144 basketball players practiced free throws. The first half physically practiced the free throws for an hour each day, while the second half mentally practiced free throws for an hour each day. And by the end of the week, both groups had actually improved the same amount. Which means, by using imagery, you can get more reps in and do less damage to your body.

For instance, in aerial skiing, a typical practice may only allow for fifteen jumps. But you can easily do fifteen jumps within a five-minute mental imagery session where you imagine yourself going through a specific movement and each muscle involved is activated. Cool, right? Your mind can build the same level of experience through imagery sessions as it would during actual physical practice!

Starting an Imagery Session

When I work with athletes, I have them start with ten minutes of progressive muscle relaxation to get into a "soft focus" before we enter into an imagery session.

To start, I have them sit down and breathe slowly. They close their eyes, inhale for four seconds, and exhale for six seconds as they progressively try to relax specific muscles. Once they have worked on their breathing, and are still, calm, and relaxed, we move into an imagery session.

When guiding athletes through an imagery exercise, I encourage them to consider all their senses. For example, I'll ask them to visualize their shoes, then pay attention to the sounds they make when coming into contact with the ground as they move. We discuss the weather and other environmental factors leading up to the beginning of a competition or game. Then, I help them imagine the sounds of the crowd, the various smells, and even the taste in their mouths. And together we replicate plays out on the field together.

Next, we delve into practice. Specifically for instances where they wish they had done better or remembered something specific. We go through it slowly, and carefully, paying attention to how the body would feel and move in that moment as we practice making the right movements. To make an imagery session truly effective, we have to be as detailed as possible. Even though you might not be consciously aware of it, you're constantly observing and experiencing your surroundings. By incorporating these intricate details into your imagery practice, you can better bridge the gap between mental creation and physical reality in your mind.

Learning to envision yourself succeeding and performing at an elite level though imagery can have a significant impact on anyone striving to improve their skills.

This strategy is consistently effective, particularly for intermediate to advanced performers. Bill Walsh, Hall of Fame coach for the San Francisco 49ers, said, "Champions act like champions long before they are champions." Imagery helps you take the first steps. Using it will allow you to quietly focus on your vision and train your body to move the way you need it to for your vision to become a reality.

Generate a Legacy

If you've tuned into my podcast, you would have heard me speak about Ken Ravizza more than a few times. In the realm of sport psychology, Ken's name is held in high regard. His contributions as a sport psychology consultant for high profile teams like the Chicago Cubs, Anaheim Angels, Florida Marlins, and Los Angeles Dodgers, and his significant role in the success of the Cal State Fullerton baseball program in the College World Series, affirm his pioneering status in our field. Sadly, Ken passed away unexpectedly at 70.

When he passed away, I witnessed an outpouring of tributes on my Twitter feed that left me feeling reflective. Despite not having a close relationship with Ken, his influence was palpable in my life. His reputation preceded him in textbooks, discussions with peers, and meeting him in 2017 only confirmed his authentic, intelligent, kind, and delightful persona.

Ken Ravizza's untimely passing led me to introspect on the legacy I'd like to leave and my role in cultivating vision, both in my life and others' lives. I ponder upon critical questions: Will I be proud of myself at life's end? Will I harbor regrets? What would I have wished to accomplish, and what would I have been proud of attempting?

Primarily, my thoughts circulate around my relationships and the imprint I leave on others. I aspire to be a father who encourages his children to dream, is present in their failures, and teaches them about persistence and courage. I aim to be an understanding and supportive parent when life gets tough. As a husband, I hope to be remembered as someone who continually evolved within the relationship. I value my wife's love and patience as I strive to exemplify resilience, tenacity, patience, and understanding. To me, relationships form the backbone of a fulfilling life.

My mission is to leave a legacy of service, healing, and compassion, inspiring others as much as I am inspired in creating uplifting content. When my time arrives, I want to be remembered for the positive impact I had on people.

What do you want to do with your legacy?

Lia Coryell, a former paralympic archery shooter and now a world cup gold medalist, shared the concept of "planting trees you'll never see." It implies investing in long-term projects that you might not see flourish in your lifetime.

Lia found hope in this concept, as a Paralympian archery shooter who suffers significantly from Multiple Sclerosis. The condition continually challenges her motor function, leading to frustration. Despite her struggles, Lia remains dedicated to leaving the world in a better state by engaging in speaking events and mentoring other archers and athletes. Her kindness, thoughtfulness, and selflessness as a world-class athlete ensure her legacy will live on.

Reflecting on your legacy is a transformative process. Begin to ponder on it, arrange your thoughts, and start working on it today. Remember, you were born for greatness, and part of that greatness involves cultivating vision and fulfilling a divine legacy that influences others for generations to come.

Produce Where You're Planted

Have you accidentally killed a houseplant before? When I ask this in a group setting, about 90% of hands in the room go up. Then I ask, why?

The answers are always the same:

1. Too much sun
2. I wasn't attentive enough
3. Not enough water

4. Not enough sun

5. Too much water

6. I didn't talk to the plant

It's not easy to raise houseplants. In my case, you might call me a serial houseplant killer. It's hard work!

Then, in the same group setting, I will ask if they know the difference between sweet corn and field corn. Believe it or not, many people don't. Especially if they're not from the midwest. Field corn, unlike sweet corn, is not sweet to the taste and is primarily fed to livestock. It's often referred to as "dented corn" and is one of the most valuable commodities produced in the US. In fact, only one percent of corn planted in the United States is sweet corn, with the remaining 99% being field corn. Because field corn has various uses, including corn cereal, corn starch, corn oil, and corn syrup production, and it is mainly used for ethanol production, livestock feed, and manufacturing goods like oils and lotions.

As America's number one field crop, corn leads all others in value and production volume. In fact, approximately thirteen billion bushels of corn are produced annually, contributing about $23.5 billion to the US economy. And the best part? This essential agricultural resource can grow in even the most challenging conditions. With minimal sunlight, water, and care, field corn continues to grow.

So which are you? A house plant or field corn? Like a house plant, do you always need help, praise, or encouragement? Or are you like field corn, and every day when you wake up you are ready to produce, regardless of the circumstances?

Mark Twain said, "I can live for two months on a good

compliment." But with a cultivated vision, you can live a lifetime of belief in yourself and your ability to bring about change, regardless of the circumstances.

Be like field corn. Wake up every day with a vision, and let this vision guide you towards your greatness. Don't wait for the validation of others; rather, let your vision propel you forward. Nurture it, believe in it, and produce where you're planted regardless of your circumstances. Do it today, and do it for you. Do it for the sake of being great!

CHALLENGE 1

Think about your legacy today. Write down some notes about what you would like your life to look like. Ask yourself the following questions:

1. What would you regret if you didn't do it or try it?
2. What would you be proud to attempt or try?
3. What are the things that matter most to you?
4. Why do you do what you do?
5. What are the characteristics of people you really admire?
6. What is the greatest compliment you could give someone?
7. What is the greatest compliment you could receive?
8. What is a tree you could plant for others that you may never see the results of?

CHALLENGE 2

What is your why? What is your calling? Do you know? Have you taken time to figure it out? It may be the most important thing you do.

This week, whether at work, on the field, try to define your why. Once you have your why defined and you understand your vision, look for specific ways you can work towards this overall vision in small moments each day. Write them down and add them to your three morning non-negotiables.

CHALLENGE 3

Find 3 tasks that help you win each day. Here are my 3. I make my bed. Every morning. No exceptions. I do the dishes. It makes my wife happy, and I get the dopamine rush of accomplishing something. And I meditate and pray. Those three items get me up. They get me going. And they get dopamine in my system early.

For yourself, identify three tasks you can do during your morning routine (aside from the obvious) that move you towards your vision as a whole.

CHAPTER 2

ENHANCE YOUR MENTAL STRENGTH

Anxiety comes easy in today's fast-paced world. Especially when we can't control everything around us. But what we often forget is that the key to enhancing your mental strength isn't found in controlling the events around you. It's found in knowing when you should let go and when you should pay attention.

A prime example of this is monkey trapping. Monkeys are fascinating creatures found in Central and South America, Africa, and Asia, with over 600 species in existence. But as captivating as they are, they can be a nuisance to local farmers. They destroy crops, steal food, and create an overall mess. Because they have been such a nuisance, farmers in third-world countries have been trapping monkeys for centuries! They simply take a coconut and cut a small hole into it, just big enough for a monkey to fit its hand through. They fill the coconut with nuts, berries, or sweets to entice the monkey. Then, they wait. Sooner or later, a monkey will come by, smell the treats, and reach inside to grab a fistful.

But here's the catch: they won't pull their hand back out while holding onto the loot, and the hole is only big enough for an empty hand.

The monkey, stubborn and unwilling to let go, is trapped. If the monkey *would* let go, it could be free. Yet it remains stuck. It grips onto its loot, refusing to release it even when farmers or other predators are near. It will even thrash about, trying to escape the trap, all the while refusing to simply open its hand.

Trying to control everything around us traps us just as easily.

What's your coconut? What are you holding onto that's keeping you from freedom in your current situation? It could be anything— politics, family, or even making money. In times of uncertainty, politics can become all-consuming, making us feel like it's the only solution to our problems. Family, though a source of love and support, can turn into a prison if we strive for unrealistic perfection. Money, essential for survival, can ensnare us when we become fixated on volatile markets instead of enjoying the process.

What are you clinging to so tightly that it has become a prison?

You have control over what you hold on to and what you let go of. Yet many of us have trouble letting go even when we know we should. We are better off when we exercise the practice of letting go. It enhances your freedom and well-being, which is why many of my clients like using the Control Circle.

The Control Circle

Control is something everyone craves. We all want to be poised in our decisions and maintain a cool, calm, and collected demeanor.

But if you try to control too much, you'll end up stressing about things you cannot change.

To help athletes separate what they can't control from what they can, I use the control circle.

Start by drawing a large circle on a piece of paper. On the outside of the circle, list the things that are beyond your control. You cannot control the people in your life, such as coaches, bosses, co-workers, teammates, opponents, politicians, and competitors. And you can't control the weather, promotions, illness, the stock market, injury, the environment, equipment, resources, venue, location, and time.

Out of all these things we just agreed we can't control, how many have you been stressed about in the past week? My guess is more than a few of these things. Unfortunately, people are often highly focused on things they cannot control, which is a large source of their stress. I argue that if you cannot control something, you should not focus on it. Actions and circumstances you can't control, while still an important influence on your life, shouldn't be something you let your thoughts linger on or try to "plan" to control in one way or another. This does nothing to aid your mental strength—it only hinders it. All you can do is accept what occurs with these people or situations and move forward with the best of your ability.

But there are absolutely things you can control.

Inside the circle, we list things under our influence of control. This includes attitude, effort, enthusiasm, nutrition, sleep, preparation, and perhaps most importantly, your reaction to circumstances. You can also control your breathing, how you frame your situation, and your gratitude. All these things are always 100% within your control.

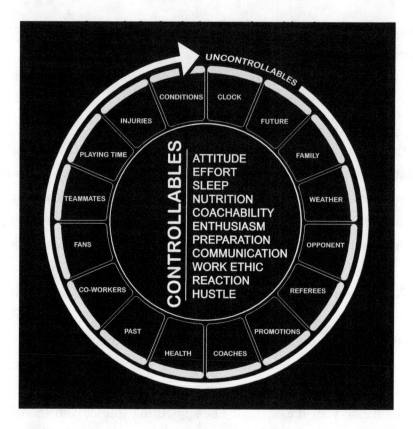

Take a moment to examine your circle. Look at the things outside and inside of it. How many of the controllable factors require God-given talent? The answer is zero. They only take planning and effort.

The key to the control circle is this: if you want to be poised, focus on the things you can control. Be hyper-focused on the controllable factors inside your circle. Control the controllables. When you dwell on things outside of the circle, you will find yourself lacking poise and stressing about things you cannot change.

Control what you can, and let go of the rest.

Take a moment to reflect on the past two weeks. What percentage of your time was spent focusing on things outside your control versus those within your control? For many people, the focus is 70% outside the circle, and 30% inside the circle. What if you made a small change? Imagine shifting just 5% more of your attention to the inside of the circle and 5% less on the outside. What impact could that make in your life?

You don't need to make a drastic change; just consistently improve your focus on what you can control.

Anxiety and stress have an inversely proportional relationship with confidence and performance. As anxiety increases, performance decreases. That is why concentrating on the inside of your control circle helps reduce anxiety. And I've seen this work on the field. One football player I work with draws a circle on his wrist as a reminder to concentrate on what he can control. The simple circle serves as a powerful reminder as the rush of the game overwhelms his senses and raises his stress levels. With the circle on his wrist, he remembers to focus on what he can control and let go of the rest.

Response

Viktor Frankl, an Auschwitz survivor, is an extraordinary example of the power of attitude in even the most dire circumstances. If he could maintain a positive mindset amidst the horrors of a concentration camp, we too can choose our attitude in our everyday lives.

In his book "Man's Search for Meaning," he wrote that between stimulus and response, there's a moment in time where we have a choice in how we respond. Whether it's five seconds or five days, we can decide how to react to any situation. Despite the Nazis taking away his clothes, health, dignity, food, and family, they could not take away his freedom to choose his reaction. This choice represents our last great freedom in life. He created a formula of stimulus + response = outcome, which is often used today. And the field of sport psychology borrowed the formula, changing it slightly to event + response = outcome (or E+R=O).

E+R=O

The formula of E+R=O is prevalent when you get into a car accident. You can't control the event, but you can control your response, which directly impacts the outcome. If your first reaction is to yell, kick your car, and cuss out the person who got into an accident with you, the outcome is likely to be worse than if you apologize (if it's your fault), check if they are hurt, and have your insurance information ready to share with them.

In this formula, the "E" stands for the event, which can be anything beyond your control—weather, traffic, an email, a loved one's behavior, or even a coach's decision. Often, these events trigger strong emotions and are influential to you.

"R" represents your reaction or response, the exciting part of the equation where you get to make choices. Minute by minute, hour by hour, you decide how to respond to events. You're the captain of your ship, in the driver's seat, with the freedom to choose. Those who excel at this take full responsibility for their actions. And the great ones—the well known athletes and those who inspire us—seem to understand that controlling their response leads to contentment and success.

"O" is the outcome. Here's some real talk: there are no guarantees. Athletes often say, "I'd be willing to do A if B happens." While I can guarantee that you'll feel better about yourself if you work harder, I can't guarantee that your coach, boss, or spouse will care. You don't control the outcome. But your response is directly related to the outcome of the event. Here is a great story about 90 seconds of poor responses which reflects this.

90 Seconds Could Cost You a Fortune

Less than three minutes into an NFL football game between the Denver Broncos and the Oakland Raiders, a fight breaks out between Broncos cornerback Aqib Talib and Raiders wide receiver Michael Crabtree. The skirmish lasts for about sixty seconds, spiraling into several other fights and delaying the game for nearly two minutes. This brief loss of control ended up costing Talib and Crabtree millions of dollars in fines and suspensions.

But why did this fight occur in the first place? It all stems from a previous game when Talib had snatched Crabtree's expensive chain necklace. The grudge they held festered for over a year, leading to the explosive altercation. This is where the fascinating science of emotions comes into play.

In this case, neither Talib or Cabtree controlled their response. When we experience a stimulus (or event), our body releases chemicals from our hypothalamus for about six seconds, affecting every living cell in our body. These chemicals are part of our regulatory function, and each burst takes between four and seven seconds to break down and be absorbed.

This is where the 90-second rule comes in. Pema Chodron introduced the concept of the 90-second rule, stating that if we allow an emotion to exist for 90 seconds without judging it, it will disappear. Though your immediate reaction to an event may be negative, you don't have to respond outwardly with negativity. Jill Bolte Taylor's book, "My Stroke of Insight: A Brain Scientist's Personal Journey[1]," takes this idea further, explaining that after the initial 90-second chemical reaction, any lingering emotions are solely our own doing. Within 90 seconds from the initial trigger, the chemical component of my anger has dissipated from my blood and my automatic response is over. If, however, I remain angry after those 90 seconds have passed, then it is because *I have chosen* to let that circuit continue to run.

Why do I share that with you? We may not really want to admit any of it, but we are responsible for how we react and regulate our emotions. That means after you have released the chemicals into your system and they have done what they showed up to do, after 90 seconds, you are feeding the fire of your own emotion. You and only you. Do you know how much damage you can do if you keep anger alive for more than 90 seconds? Michael Crabtree and Aqib Talib had kept it alive for over a year, and they lost millions of dollars in just ten seconds.

Even if your initial reaction is negative, you need to give yourself space to understand that reaction. Accept it and move on. If you let an emotion consume you, and you are unable to control how you react, you likely won't get a good outcome. This is where behavioral strategies like Acceptance Commitment Therapy (ACT) can help us.

---

1   (Taylor, 2009)

Acceptance and Commitment Therapy (ACT)

Russ Harris wrote a book called "The Happiness Trap" which acts as a guide to Acceptance and Commitment Therapy (ACT). His goal is to help patients focus on mindfulness so they can reduce stress and overcome fear, overall creating an abundant life. When he explains ACT, he says, "Acceptance and Commitment Therapy is based upon six core principles that work together to help you develop a life-changing mindset known as psychological flexibility[2]." He goes on to explain these six principles—diffusion, expansion, connection, the observing self, values, and committed action—which help you diffuse negative emotions and move forward.

ACT, to me, is about recognizing our thoughts and emotions and allowing ourselves to sit with them so that they can dissipate naturally. Have you ever found yourself feeling anxious about being anxious, or nervous about being nervous? The goal of ACT is to identify these emotions, label what you're feeling and thinking, and give the emotional fire a chance to burn out on its own. This is how we can better control our responses.

ACT has helped me on a regular basis. For instance, during the COVID-19 pandemic starting in 2020, I worked closely with a group of nurses in the Seattle area to help them manage anxiety and stress. As I listened to their hardships, I recognized that I started to feel anxious myself. Using ACT, I decided to embrace the discomfort and give myself a time limit of forty-five minutes to experience these feelings. I drove to my favorite overlook of the Salt Lake City valley to decompress and label my anxiety, delving specifically into why

---

2   (Harris, 2016)

I felt the way I did. I labeled my thoughts and emotions in a non-judgmental manner, simply recognizing that they were present.

After just fifteen minutes, my anxiety had subsided, and I no longer needed the full forty-five minutes to decompress.

Power of Your Words

As you begin taking space to feel your feelings and control your responses, it's important to note the power words hold over you. Even if they are only internal thoughts, they affect our ability to achieve the desired reaction to an event. The best thing to remember is that not all of our thoughts are true. Even if they seem true. Many inaccurate thought processes can derail our confidence and our understanding of reality. This is why we need to be aware of how we speak to ourselves.

Awareness is perhaps the most powerful seed to unlocking mental toughness. Once we've identified inaccurate thought processes, a powerful next step is to transform them into more accurate and truthful thoughts. You can do this by shaping the way you think about failure differently.

As a parent, a coach, or a leader in an organization, you can turn any "loss" into a win by focusing on the bravery and courage of the moment. For example, try using words like "brave" and "courageous" when describing or thinking about failures. For every shortfall, think about the bravery and courage it took to make the attempt at all. Even if that attempt ended in failure. Remind yourself and others around you it takes guts to try.

I use this approach with my kids frequently. When my son made a game-winning shot, I focused on the bravery and courage it took to take that shot, encouraging him to be happy with the result regardless of the outcome. And when I persuaded my daughter to attempt a front flip of the diving board, only to see her "fail" with a belly flop, I praised her bravery and courage for trusting me and taking the leap.

This mindset is useful when handling failure.

Remember to emphasize to yourself the bravery and courage it took you to try. Even if the outcome wasn't what you hoped it would be, It doesn't mean you failed; it means you were vulnerable enough to put yourself out there. Confidence is achieved by being brave and courageous, even when scared. After all, the bravest people in the world aren't without fear; they are oftentimes the ones who simply stay brave a few moments longer than the rest of us.

Enthusiasm

The power of enthusiasm is well-understood among those who have achieved greatness. Everyone knows both an Eeyore and a Tigger in their life. I bet two names came to mind just as you read those words. And when each of these people call your phone, you likely have a different reaction. The Eeyore, with their gloomy and depressive demeanor, certainly has their challenges, and you only have space for them every once in a while. Yet, when the Tigger—the bundle of positivity and infectious energy—calls, you're more inclined to answer. When Tigger bounds into your life, asking if you want to see how high he can jump, you can't help but share in his excitement.

My son, Jack, beautifully illustrates this idea of contagious enthusiasm. A few years ago, I had to bring him along to a presentation I gave to a volleyball club. Armed with his iPad and books, Jack was as good as gold at the back of the room. When I got to the part of my presentation about Tiggers in our life, I pointed to Jack. I said, "Hey,

Jack! Could you show us how fast you can run in your new shoes?" Jack's excitement was palpable as he jumped up and darted around the room, brimming with joy and pride. His energy didn't end there—he proceeded to jump around the room, further spreading his infectious positivity. Everyone in that room was uplifted by Jack's energy, and it beautifully demonstrated the contagious nature of enthusiasm.

Unfortunately, Eeyore's gloom is contagious too. The mindset, mood, and enthusiasm we bring to our lives can spread to those around us. When you think of the people you admire—the successful athletes, the accomplished musicians, the community leaders, and the hard workers—don't they all have a unique energy and enthusiasm that make them attractive? This is the power of cultivating and radiating enthusiasm.

Like field corn that continues to grow regardless of the circumstances, allow your enthusiasm to remain unwavering. Let it fuel your vision, driving you to wake up every day with the readiness to produce and grow. That's what the great ones do. They harness their unique, contagious energy, and it's this energy that propels them to the highest peaks of their careers and lives. So, what kind of energy are you spreading? What will others catch from you? Remember, cultivating an infectious enthusiasm can lead you towards your path to greatness. Be the Tigger in someone's life and watch how far it takes you.

How Do We Fix Negative Thinking?

In Dr. Shad Helmstetter's insightful book, "What to Say When You Talk to Yourself," he presents a startling statistic: researchers have found that 77% of our thoughts are negative, counterproductive, and work against us. Furthermore, research shows that we have approximately sixty-six thousand to eighty thousand thoughts per day. Using the previous statistics, and if we take the lower number of the sixty-six thousand thoughts to task, that means we bombard ourselves with fifty thousand negative or counterproductive thoughts per day!

Crazy, right?

With so much negativity ingrained in our minds, it's no wonder we struggle to change the harmful neural pathways that have developed over time. According to these stats, over 75% of the time, we are essentially programming ourselves for sickness and failure. It's a heart-wrenching statistic that affects not only ourselves but those around us.

So now the big question, how do we fix our negative thinking? Here are a few methods to try:

1. Eliminate "Catastrophizers"

To start, let's put an end to dealing in "catastrophizers" or words that are extreme and dramatic words like "always," "never," and "every time," which often distort reality. These words are known as absolutes, and by recognizing and eliminating these terms from our vocabulary, we can create a more accurate and balanced perspective on life.

When we say things like "I always fail at this," or "I'll never get that promotion," we're unconsciously setting up barriers in our mind and programming ourselves for failure or disappointment. They make us doubt our abilities, boxing us into a space where growth cannot happen, which then creates a restrictive narrative that blocks progress. They constrain our perception of reality, restricting us from exploring the possibilities that lie beyond.

The worst part is, these words are rarely grounded in absolute truth. Sure, you may have faced setbacks or failures in the past, but that doesn't mean you're doomed to fail. Yes, that promotion might be a challenging goal, but to assert that you'll never achieve it completely disregards your potential for growth and improvement. These limiting words can have particularly damaging effects in contexts such as sports and the workplace, where mindset and attitude are key determinants of success. For instance, a basketball player who convinces themselves they "always" miss crucial shots likely will. And, an employee who believes they are "never" recognized for their work may start to underperform, making their belief a reality.

Don't fall into this trap. Absolutes can be harmful when you use them in your self-talk. If you catch yourself using them, pause, and remind yourself that they may not be the truth.

2. Surround Yourself with Optimistic People

Another way to combat negativity is by surrounding ourselves with optimistic people who can lift our spirits and encourage a brighter outlook. These individuals, like my Grandpa Clark, know how to acknowledge difficulties while highlighting the beauty in life, leaving us feeling uplifted and positive. Be mindful, however, of the difference between genuine optimism and toxic positivity, which lacks empathy and can be harmful to our mental health.

3. Choose Empowering Vocabulary

It's essential to be mindful of the vocabulary we use. By choosing empowering and uplifting words, we can create a positive atmosphere for ourselves and those around us. In the words of John F. Kennedy, "A rising tide lifts all boats."

4. Immerse Yourself in Positivity

Immerse yourself in positivity by reading uplifting books, following inspiring people, and listening to motivational podcasts. With the wealth of resources available, you can fill your mind with positive influences and, in turn, become an influencer of positivity in others' lives.

5. Control the Controllables

It's also vital to focus on controlling the controllables in life, such as sleep, nutrition, attitude, and preparation. Remember your control circle and let go of what you cannot control, like the weather, politics, and other people's perceptions, and leave them to a higher power.

6. Look for the Good

Make a conscious effort to look for the good in life. When you search for positivity, you'll be surprised to find it everywhere around you. Every smile from a stranger, every person who opens a door or asks how your day is going added to the positivity counter. It shows you how much positivity is actively within a world where it's easy to only see the negative.

7. Choose Positivity in Every Response

Choose positivity by minding the gap between events and responses. In that gap lies your power to choose how you respond, so opt for a positive reaction every time.

Negative thinking can consume us and get in our way personally and professionally. A large aspect of enhancing your mental strength means recognizing when your thoughts may be negative and pulling yourself out of them. This doesn't mean you are not allowed to ever have negative thoughts. They come to all of us. But, you can recognize them and know they are not helpful to your success.

Shake It Off and Step Up

Developing a strong sense of focus is essential for achieving greatness in any aspect of life. To be good, you must *see* the good.

We give power to what we focus on. When working with a team, I often ask the coach to send one of their team members multiple texts during the presentation. The team doesn't know I've made this ask. Inevitably, during my presentation, someone will get a ping on their phone and look down at it instead of concentrating on the information being presented to them. And they might even be unable to resist the urge to respond to said text.

This lack of focus is not unique to athletes—it's a widespread issue in today's world. Recent studies show that most of us can only go as long as six minutes without interruption to our focus. Which is part of the reason why people often fail to practice focus, allowing distractions to pull them away from their goals and objectives. When someone enters a room late, it's common for people to glance at the newcomer rather than continue paying attention to the speaker. Don't let distractions ruin your concentration. Whether in a lesson, or while practicing a sport, keep your goal in mind. Focus is key to your success.

By practicing focus, you can train yourself to resist distractions and stay attentive to what truly matters. Kobe Bryant understood this as well. He frequently used meditation and mindfulness to improve his focus. This mindfulness helped him see obstacles as a challenge, rather than something he couldn't get past. With the slew of challenges and distractions he faced, I don't think he would have had the career he had if he didn't know how to tackle obstacles with an open mind. Kobe Bryant could truly "Shake it off and step up."

This saying comes from the parable of the mule who fell in the well. One day, a farmer heard his mule crying out for help. Upon investigating, he discovered that the mule had fallen into his old well. The farmer sympathized with the mule but concluded that neither the mule nor the well was worth saving. So, he called his neighbors for help to bury the mule in the well and end its misery.

Initially, the old mule was completely hysterical! Wouldn't you be? I can't imagine the thought of being buried alive in a well. But as the farmer and his neighbors continued shoveling, and dirt hit the mule's back, a simple thought struck the old mule. It dawned on him that every time a shovel load of dirt landed on his back, he should shake it off and step up!

Over and over, the mule repeated this mantra, facing each painful blow of dirt with determination. Despite the seemingly hopeless circumstances, the mule continued to shake off the dirt and step up. Eventually, battered and exhausted, the mule triumphed, stepping over the wall of the well to freedom. What initially appeared to be its doom had become its salvation, all thanks to the mule's focus during a dire situation.

Often, the adversities we face in life have the potential to benefit and bless us, provided we reframe our perspective and rise to the occasion. We cannot do that unless we focus on the task at hand with an open mind.

Do you feel like you're being buried alive by a situation in your life? Are you overwhelmed with emotions or feeling hopeless and out of control?

Remember, everything can work together for the greater good if we seek out the positive in every situation. This doesn't mean that we don't see the situation for what it is; rather, we focus on a better and more helpful outcome. The more we *focus* on something, the more power we give it. Just like the mule, we too can shake off the dirt and step up to overcome life's challenges.

Looking at a dark situation with the understanding that you can make it better can be a difficult trick. Here are five strategies to help:

1. **Simplify:** Often, we complicate our lives by overthinking situations. The fundamentals of your job, family life, and team can always be simplified. Remember that there is a solution for every problem, even if it takes longer or is more difficult than anticipated. Keep things straightforward and focus on finding solutions rather than dwelling on complexities.

2. **Work backwards from long-term goals:** Breaking down your goals into smaller, daily tasks is a powerful way to achieve success. By focusing on these smaller objectives, you build confidence and make progress each day. Just like in sports, life has its fundamentals—what are your daily fundamentals that contribute to your long-term goals?

3. **Ask yourself "why":** Understanding the reasons behind your hard work and goals is crucial for self-improvement. Discovering your "why" provides you with a purpose that helps you face each day with determination. Sometimes, asking "why not" can also

be transformative—why not you? Why not now? Remember, you can do hard things.

4. **Write down your ideas and solutions:** Inspiration and clarity can strike at unexpected moments. Keep a small notebook or use the notes app on your phone to record these insights. This habit can be incredibly uplifting and helpful when dealing with adversity.

5. **Hone your listening skills:** Do you have a mentor who can offer honest guidance? If not, seek one out. In our fast-paced, multitasking world, it's essential to focus on active listening skills to address challenges and work more efficiently. Being a good listener is a lost art, and mastering this skill can provide valuable information to improve your craft.

When you focus on what you can control, your mental strength skyrockets. Remember, the difference between the good and the great is that the great understand these principles and apply them daily.

CHALLENGE 1

Create and fill out your own circle of control. Put it up somewhere where you regularly see it. Additionally, here are seven ways to fix negative thinking. Pick at least three of these and start implementing them today to gain more control over the negativity in your mind.

1. Eliminate "catastrophizers."
2. Surround yourself with optimistic people.
3. Choose empowering vocabulary.
4. Immerse yourself in positivity.
5. Control the controllables.

6. Look for the good.

7. Choose positivity in every response.

CHALLENGE 2

Imagine a hallway full of emotions and truths you have accepted as reality. Take them off the shelf, dust them off, and see if they are good for you. Ask where they came from. Ask if they really *are* true and if they are working for you or against you. If they are working against you, toss them out, flush them, and make room for good things which build, rather than the negative things which fester. If the emotions or "truths" are problematic, release them. Use a reset routine to get rid of them for good.

CHAPTER 3

GRIT

In our society, it's all too common to equate intelligence and talent with success. We tend to idolize people who have natural born talent. We feel that if we're not one of them, we don't stand a chance at achieving greatness. But the truth is, success is not solely determined by the gifts we are born with.

Have you ever heard of the marshmallow test? It was a study published in Psychological Science where eight-year-old children were placed in front of a marshmallow and asked to wait to eat it. If they did, they would get a reward. Some kids ate the marshmallow quickly, others waited until told they could eat the marshmallows. They followed these children through the years, finding the ones who could put off good for great were the ones who were more successful in most areas of their life such as jobs, skills, and relationships.

The science is clear: resilience and grit are much more important factors in achieving our goals than innate talent. Grit is the embodiment of tenacity, determination, and moxie. It is a key predictor of success in various areas of life, including sports, business, and education. Grit has been shown to be more important than talent or intelligence.

Angela Duckworth's groundbreaking book, "Grit," beautifully illustrates the power of grit as a key factor in accomplishment. Duckworth poses that our most important talent might not be a particular skill or intelligence, but rather a talent for working hard. Duckworth defines grit: "Grit is passion and perseverance for very long-term goals. Grit is having stamina. Grit is sticking with your future, day in, day out, not just for the week, not just for the month, but for years, and working really hard to make that future a reality. Grit is living life like it's a marathon, not a sprint[1]." By embracing grit, you can unlock your potential for greatness, regardless of the natural talents you may possess.

Grit In Action

How do we identify grit? Mental performance coach Justin Su'a, who helps the Tampa Bay Rays, can often be heard saying, "Little by little, a little becomes a lot."

During a flight, a good pilot makes small course corrections to the flight path to ensure the plane arrives at its destination. He does not need to overcorrect. A few degrees to the right and to the left keeps the plane on track. It's the same with us. If we make small corrections and course changes daily, we will stay on course for our destination. This method is even found in scripture. Alma 37:6-7 (Book of Mormon) says, "By small and simple things are great things brought to pass[2]."

Marginal improvements can have a massive impact. It takes grit to keep going when improvement can only be seen on a microscopic level.

---

1   (Duckworth A. , 2018)
2   (Mormon, 1830)

The science is clear that these traits were positively associated with performance in athletes.[3] Grit is also a better predictor of performance than talent or physical ability, in all things.[4] Grit has also significantly predicted athletic success and mental toughness in NCAA Division athletes.[5]

We typically want big changes for our hard work. But grit can be identified when you see professional athletes working on marginal improvements consistently. Even if the reward of that work isn't obvious, they are still on the court or field practicing the same swing, hit, catch, or throw day after day to improve their skills.

Here are a few real-life examples of grit in the big leagues:

1. Despite a life-threatening blood clot in her lungs in 2011, Serena Williams worked tirelessly to regain her strength and stamina. Her grit and determination led her to win her fifth Wimbledon championship in 2012 and since then has surely secured her place as one of the greatest tennis players of all time.

2. Although drafted in the sixth round of the NFL draft, Tom Brady refused to let his critics define him. Through hard work and dedication, he became one of the greatest quarterbacks in NFL history, winning seven Super Bowl championships.

3. Known for her incredible athleticism and skill, Simone Biles faced immense pressure as the favorite to win multiple gold medals in the 2016 Olympics. Despite injuries, Biles performed flawlessly on the balance beam and went on to win four gold

---

3   (Gucciardi, Hanton, & Mallett, 2012)

4   (Duckworth H. , 2016)

5   (Lantz, Michel, & Glickman, 2018)

medals and one bronze. Simone has mentioned numerous times, "It feels weird if I'm not in pain."

Athletes like Serena Williams, Tom Brady, and Simone Biles knew their "why" and pushed through challenges because they had developed mental toughness in the face of adversity. Without this, they likely wouldn't have reached the status they have achieved today.

Overcoming Adversity

Every great team, every great organization, and every great individual I have ever worked with experiences some sort of adversity every year. Adversity is an inevitable part of life, and it can come in various shapes and sizes. Whether it's a slow, dull pain or a sharp, sudden bite, it often causes hurt, fear, and anxiety. And the great ones I work with always have a plan to overcome adversity when it steps onto their path.

One of the ways they overcome anxiety is by practicing good body language when things aren't going their way. The science is clear: body language has a direct impact on self-talk, and self-talk has a direct impact on body language. They understand both are entwined together, and both need to be positive. They also focus on the next item of business. In an organization, on a team, or as an individual, the next "play" is the most important one.

A great team may focus on effort and compliments rather than schemes when it comes to pressure moments. Keeping it simple and productive is a great "game time" decision. Sometimes it is important to realize that having a plan is the best way to stay positive. Simply put, positive people are positive because they have a plan and they are working it.

One of my favorite quotes about adversity comes from Thomas S. Monson's 2013 address "I Will Not Fail Thee, nor Forsake Thee." He says, "Good timber does not grow with ease. The stronger the wind, the stronger the trees. The further the sky, the greater the length. The more the storm, the more the strength. By sun and cold, by rain and snow. In trees and men, good timbers grow."[6]

In addition, the University of Arizona's "Biosphere 2" study offers an intriguing lesson about the importance of adversity in our lives. Researchers studied trees, rivers, fruits, vegetables, and other aspects of the ecosystem in the biosphere, but they found something interesting happening with the trees. The trees in the biosphere grew faster than those in the wild, never fully matured. Eventually, they would collapse under their own weight. The reason for this was the absence of wind in the biosphere, which, as it turns out, plays a crucial role in a tree's life.

When plants and trees grow in the wild, the constant movement caused by the wind creates stress in the tree's wooden load-bearing structure. To compensate, the tree produces reaction wood (or stress wood), which has a different structure than its regular wood and allows the tree to position itself for optimal light and resources. This stress wood enables trees to grow in a more solid manner, contort towards the best light, and survive even in awkward shapes. In essence, the presence of wind, and the stress it causes, makes the tree stronger.

For those of you going through tough times, know you are not alone. There are countless people facing their own challenges, and together, we can find the strength to prevail. But it is the presence of those challenges that makes our resolve stronger. If you're not

---

6   (Monson, 2013)

currently experiencing adversity, reflect on past experiences that tested your resolve. Think about the strategies and support systems that helped you overcome these challenges.

When facing adversity, ask yourself these questions:

- What will this teach me?
- How did I get here, and what caused this to happen?
- What is the outcome I want the most?
- What other outcomes would be good as well?
- What stands in my way from making these outcomes happen?
- Who do I know that has overcome similar obstacles?
- Will this problem stress me out in five years? If not, it's probably a good idea not to put too much energy into it.

Embrace the Suck

Have you ever been to a bamboo forest?

In group settings, I often ask if anyone knows how long it takes to grow a bamboo forest. Typically, someone might say, "Oh, it takes an incredibly long time. Like, five years for a bamboo forest to grow." Another might counter, "I heard it's very short. Bamboo trees grow from zero to 90 feet in about six weeks." The truth is, both of these observations are correct.

Growing a bamboo forest does take a long time because the bamboo tree doesn't break through the surface for five years. You have to water it, give it sunlight, apply different fertilizers, and wait. Even after the first couple years, it won't poke through the surface, but you have to keep maintaining and watering it. Then, almost to the day of year five, the first bamboo shoots push through the surface. And six weeks later, you'll have an entire forest of bamboo standing about 90 feet tall. Crazy right? How easy would it be to give up on the process of watering and fertilizing dirt during those five years? Especially when you don't see any results.

Could you keep faith that the bamboo trees would grow without any signs of change? Many times the great ones have experienced progress like this. We don't know who they are, until something happens—a fantastic play or a game-winning shot—then suddenly everyone knows who they are. We didn't see the silent growth in the background; we just saw the success. Lionel Messi became indignant when fans called him an overnight success. He said, "I wasn't an overnight success. It has taken me seventeen years, six months, twenty-seven days, and four hours to become the soccer player you see today."

Those seventeen years weren't filled with fame and recognition. They were filled with hard work and likely a lot of hard moments. But without embracing those moments, we likely wouldn't know Lionel Messi's name. Embracing the suck is an essential part of overcoming adversity and developing grit. Every person in every organization experiences some form of adversity each year. You should expect adversity to come your way so you aren't surprised by it and so you can plan on how to handle it.

My grandfather used to tell great stories and jokes when I was young. And one stands out as a reminder of what can happen when we let adversity consume us and control our emotions.

The story tells of a traveling salesman who gets a flat tire out in the country in the heat of the day. As he searches through his trunk, he removes all his sales folders, materials, and widgets. Now, as a traveling salesman, he lives out of his car, so this takes a generous amount of time. Once he has finally reached the bottom of his trunk, he is drenched in sweat and realizes he has a tire iron and a lug wrench, but no jack to repair his flat tire.

Annoyed, he sits on the back of his car thinking about his next move, and he sees a light about a mile in the distance. The sun is setting at this point, so the salesman puts all his hope into the idea that the farmer in the distance will have a jack.

He travels toward the light, feet hurting, kicking rocks on the way, and arrives at the door. He knocks. Then he knocks again. No answer.

The salesman, now even more frustrated, leaves the porch and ponders his next move. He is pretty sure someone was at the residence where he was knocking, and he's irritated they didn't answer the door. As he continues walking, he curses into the night and continues another mile to the next residence.

Again, no answer. Again, the frustration of the salesman mounts. In anger, he kicks the door and shouts, "Are you kidding me?!!"

He then continues farther down the road and sees another residence. However, his anger and frustration is boiling within him. This anger is taking over his thoughts completely, and he begins talking to himself, "I'll bet you this guy doesn't answer either. I'll bet you he's not willing to help me. I can't stand this area of the country. I can't stand these people. I can't stand my job. This is ridiculous!"

Then, as he comes to the front of the third porch, he knocks, and to his surprise, an older farmer answers the door, with a jack in his hand. With a big smile the farmer says, "I bet you have a flat tire and need some help."

But the salesman, too angry and consumed with his own thoughts, punches the farmer in the face and says, "I didn't want your damn jack anyway."

I tell this story because this is the story of an athlete, a salesman, a parent, and a CEO or anyone else who has become frustrated and reacted poorly due to their boiling emotions. The Green Berets[7] say, "Embrace the suck, don't stay in the suck." Meaning you should face adversity head-on, but don't allow yourself to be consumed by it. Allowing yourself to be consumed often makes the situation worse, just like it did for the traveling salesman.

This story holds several lessons for anyone facing adversity:

1. Manage your self-talk: When negative thoughts start to spiral out of control, use a keyword or phrase to calm yourself down. Words like "pause," "stop," and "quit" can help you regain control and prevent impulsive actions.

2. Express gratitude: Make an effort to thank coworkers, bosses, teammates, coaches, or anyone else who has helped you along the way. Gratitude can make a significant difference in your relationships and overall well-being.

3. Be patient and persistent as a leader: If you are a mentor, coach, or leader, understand that you may face resistance from time to time. Be patient and continue to help and lead, even if others' attitudes are challenging. You may not know their complete story, but your persistence can have a lasting impact on their lives.

Remember the story of Talib and Crabtree, and how they lost millions in just 90 seconds? They didn't embrace the suck. They were consumed by it.

---

7   The United States Army Special Forces

Embracing the suck is a crucial aspect of overcoming adversity and building resilience. By facing challenges head-on and maintaining a healthy perspective, you can prevent negative self-talk and emotions from controlling your actions. Embracing the suck allows you to learn from adversity, cultivate gratitude, and grow stronger as a leader. By doing so, you become more capable of handling future challenges. Instead of allowing the suck to control you, transform it into a catalyst for growth and personal development.

Breathe Until You Find Clarity

One of your biggest tools to overcome adversity is learning how to breathe so you can maintain calm and focus.

BREATHE TO RELIEVE
4 COMPONENTS TO DEEP BREATHING
(ADAPTED FROM MARK CHENEY, CMPC)

01 BREATHE THROUGH THE NOSE

THIS WARMS, FILTERS, AND MOISTENS THE AIR. IT ALSO PRODUCES NITRIC OXIDE, WHICH BENEFITS THE CARDIOVASCULAR SYSTEM

02 DIAPHRAGMATIC BREATHING

DIAPHRAGMATIC BREATHING FILLS THE LUNGS MORE COMPLETELY THAN CHEST BREATHING. IT ALSO STIMULATES THE VAGUS NERVE, GENERATING A SENSE OF CALM.

03 MAKE IT RYTHMIC

TAKING FOUR SECONDS TO INHALE, AND SIX SECONDS TO EXHALE DECREASES THE HEART RATE, MUSCLE TENSION, AND STRESS.

04 USE IMAGERY TO HELP

IN WITH THE BLUE, OUT WITH THE RED. IMAGINE COOL CRISP REFRESHING, CLEAN AIR ON THE INHALE. NOW IMAGINE HOT STRESS AND TENSION LEAVING THE BODY, LIKE A DRAGONS BREATH AS YOU EXHALE.

Remember the football player who drew a circle on his wrist? He also drew a box on the other wrist to symbolize box breathing—a proven method for reducing anxiety and promoting focus. By breathing through your nose, you can create nitrous oxide, which enhances your cardiovascular ability to deliver oxygen throughout your body, particularly to the extremities used in sports. Here is a graphic explaining how to breathe efficiently for adversity:

Breathing like this allows you to expand and massage the vagus nerve. This nerve, running along the inside of your backbone, has been linked to feelings of calmness, clarity, and confidence when stimulated through deep breaths. By massaging it with this breathing technique, you activate these feelings. Which is why you should try to incorporate this breathing technique when a play goes wrong, you have failed a project, or someone has disappointed you—it helps you regain control and confidence before offering a response.

Influencing Grit

If you feel you lack grit or mental toughness, there are strategies to develop greater resilience. Inc Magazine recently highlighted various studies on grit, revealing key factors that contribute to the resilience of individuals who persevere through difficult times. Here are some findings which show how the most resilient among us keep going despite incredibly trying times:

1. They face fear
2. They have a high moral compass
3. They draw upon faith
4. They draw upon social support
5. They have good role models
6. They are physically fit
7. They make sure their brains are challenged
8. They have cognitive and emotional flexibility
9. They have meaning, purpose, and growth in life
10. They have realistic optimism

The good news? Many of these characteristics can be cultivated through mindfulness. In fact, Martin Seligman, the father of "positive psychology," has developed a program that promotes conscious awareness of thoughts and the ability to challenge those thoughts by considering alternatives. Through mindfulness, you can change thoughts from "My boss just ignored me in the hallway because she hates my guts," to "My boss likely didn't see me in the hallway."

But mindfulness isn't the only way to bring these key factors of grittiness into our lives. We can also do so with a focus on mindset and purpose.

Mindset and Purpose

Individuals with a growth mindset believe their abilities can be advanced through hard work, and individuals with a clear sense of purpose are driven by a deep understanding of their "why."

These two factors give you more moxie than you could imagine.

A study published in the Journal of Research in Personality [8]found people with a strong sense of purpose tend to be more resilient and less prone to depression and anxiety.

When it comes to mindset, the first person I think of is a good friend of mine from the Snow College football team. John South played wide receiver with me at Snow College, and that year, we happened to have two other fantastic wide receivers who went on to play professionally in the SEC and the NFL. And because of their talent, my friend was buried beneath them on the charts. In three years of college, he never made the traveling squad and only dressed for home games. But every week, he would still hustle relentlessly. He outpaced

---

8   (Morin, 7 Scientifically Proven Benefits of Gratitude, 2015)

us all, worked hard consistently, and didn't let the circumstance stop him from getting better.

At the end of the year during a game, we were winning, and I talked the coach into letting my friend play. He got a great catch that game, which happened to be his only catch at Snow College.

Is that where the story ends?

No. He received a walk-on tryout to Utah State, but the person running the tryouts mocked him, asking for a "real receiver." Of course, this insulted my friend, as it would insult anybody, but instead he kept looking for his next opportunity. All the while, he kept practicing. Eventually, he transferred to Adams State. And from there he went on to be a two time All-Conference performer, and an All-American at Adams State. He had 62 catches his junior year with over 1,100 yards receiving with an average of 127.9 yards per game! This was a guy who didn't even make it on the field at Snow College. He was mocked and teased. Yet, all he did in the face of adversity was put his head down and continue to work.

Purpose and mindset went hand in hand for my friend as he moved through his college career. Without being ruled by those two key concepts, he might not have had the grit to keep going. Grit is achievable and within your reach. All you have to do is stretch out and grab it.

CHALLENGE 1

Practice breathing the next time you make a mistake or feel you are losing your patience. Breathe in through your nose for 4 seconds, and out through your mouth as if you are blowing through a straw for 6 seconds. After three deep breaths this way, you should feel a powerful calming effect. Repeat it throughout the day as needed. It's the best thing you can do, in a heated moment, to refocus on the task at hand.

CHALLENGE 2

For those of you having a hard time, find the courage today to do the work. Get busy and stop feeling sorry for yourself. That doesn't mean your adversity isn't real or unfair, but the way to get out of the funk is to do the work. When it's tough, keep going. If you feel like quitting, press on. As the saying goes, "The good Lord can't steer a parked car." When they tell you that you can't do it, ignore them. This exact storm you are facing may be the next step to achieving your full potential.

PART 2

MOTIVATIONAL DETERRENTS

When it comes to motivation, we often find ourselves battling against three major roadblocks: comparison, perfectionism, and unrealistic expectations.

You see, when our ancient predecessors ventured around the corner of a rock, three things could happen. First, nothing. Second, they found something to eat. And third, a sabertooth tiger ate them. Our brains evolved with an alarm system to protect us in these situations—the amygdala. It's constantly on guard, making sure we're safe. But when that alarm goes off, good decision-making can take a backseat.

I had an experience like this of my own. One night, I went through my usual routine of helping my kids get ready for bed— brushing their teeth, putting on their pajamas, and tucking them in with prayer, stories, and snuggles. After saying goodnight, I joined my wife in our room and went to sleep.

At 2:47 a.m., I was jolted awake by our pre-alarm system (courtesy of Vivint) kindly warning that if not deactivated within thirty seconds, the main alarm would start blaring. My initial thoughts were, "Why on earth is this alarm going off?" As I grumbled out of bed, irritation clouded my judgment for a brief moment as I marched to the kitchen to silence the alarm. I couldn't help but think about how annoying it was to be woken up like this. My wife whispered, asking what I was doing. That's when it hit me: our alarm had never given a false alert in the nine years we've had it. Suddenly, I realized this wasn't a false alarm, and the main alarm began to wail throughout our home and neighborhood.

The piercing sound of the alarm, coupled with my groggy and disoriented state, made it incredibly challenging to think clearly. But as I realized the situation, the college football player in me took over and I sprinted to my children's rooms ready to wreak havoc on anything and anyone who got in my way.

To my surprise, they were fast asleep, despite the deafening alarm. I kissed their foreheads and went to check the alarm panel, which indicated an intrusion at the back door. I went downstairs and found the door unlocked and slightly open, likely from our kids going in and out during the day. Perhaps the wind had opened it wider and set the alarm off. When I discussed this potential with my wife, we decided to review the footage from the security camera in my home office. I always have one on for me and my clients' safety, and the office happens to be located next to the back door.

What we saw was chilling. A shadowy figure entered our home, walked past the office camera, and then quickly fled when the alarm went off. Just a few seconds later, I had been standing in the very same spot. To this day, I still shiver when I think about it. Because panic took over, I had barely missed an intruder in our house who could have done harm to me and my family during that time.

When strong emotions overtake us, it's difficult to see clearly.

This brings us to the performance paradox of sport. As Ralph Vernacchia said, "The better an athlete gets, the more he or she may fail."[1] As athletes approach their performance ceiling, improvements become smaller and harder to achieve. Consequently, it's increasingly difficult to recognize small wins and easier to focus on failures.

And guess what starts going off? That's right, alarm bells. It's then that motivation begins to tank and frustration builds. Our judgment gets clouded, and we think maybe we shouldn't do this difficult thing *at all.*

I currently work with Patrick Fishburn, a player on the Korn Ferry Golf Tour. When we started working together, he was ranked in the 90s on the tour, which is lower amongst his peers. But after some time together, he moved up to 26th—just one stroke away from earning his PGA tour card! This was a huge leap in ranking for him. But the most exciting part? To make this drastic change, Patrick only needed to improve *0.2 strokes per round.*

What was the end result of this situation? Was he frustrated? Did he make it? How does it exemplify what you were stating before? Did he not see the progress? Hint: He just received his PGA tour card in 2023. His average strokes per round went up from 69.75 (2022) to 68.96 (2023) or an improvement year to year of just *.79 strokes per round!*

Patrick was able to make progress when improvement is hard to see. It's easy to beat ourselves up and get impatient, our alarm bells go off, and we lose motivation. This is often when comparison, perfectionism, and unrealistic expectations creep up on us. These

---

1   (Vernacchia, 2003)

three motivational deterrents block us from reaching our full potential and make high level performance nearly impossible. You need tools to overcome them.

The next section of the book is adapted from the writings of Dr. Keith Henschen and Dr. Nicole Detling, and will be dedicated to identifying and overcoming these deterrents so you can keep motivated and stay courageous whenever you experience adversity.

CHAPTER 4

COMPARISON

Our world revolves around comparisons. Especially as social media has risen to the forefront of our lives. And among the likes, emojis, and comments, we tend to forget that comparison is for *things*, not people.

The only person you should compare yourself to is the person you were yesterday. My mother always told me, "Comparison is a tool of the devil," and I agree with her. While comparing similarities and dissimilarities between two things can be beneficial, using comparison as a measure of our own self-worth is destructive and de-motivating. "Comparison is the thief of joy," according to Teddy Roosevelt, and in my work, I've never found him to be wrong.

Our Current Struggle with Comparison

Comparison has become increasingly difficult for the current generation.

We live in a society which constantly compares people, and with the prevalence of smartphones, we can't help but be bombarded by others' Instagram, Twitter, and TikTok feeds. What we see, however, is a carefully curated highlight reel of people's lives, rarely showcasing the struggles and bad days that everyone experiences. As a result, we end up comparing our average (or bad) days to someone else's highlight reel.

Which is a recipe for disaster.

In high school, I played quarterback, point guard, and I was a shortstop on the baseball team. You might have thought I was popular, but the truth is, there were many Friday and Saturday nights when I stayed home. Can you imagine how discouraged I would have been if I knew about the events others held without me? They undoubtedly happened, but I was blissfully unaware and didn't worry about them. But nowadays, kids tend to remain very aware. Due to social media, they know about every event they aren't invited to. And, understandably, that makes them feel like they aren't good enough.

Then begins the comparison cycle. We think, maybe if I had a better car, or was friends with a specific person, or didn't do that really embarrassing thing at lunch, I would have been invited. And this extends past high school into our professional and private lives. We see the accomplishments others make, or the things they buy, and berate ourselves for not having the same or better.

Comparison is for the buying stage when you need to choose between a house or a car. It should be reserved for decisions like which university to go to and which job offer to take. But it should not be used when looking at other people.

Recent national statistics reveal alarming connections between depression and anxiety of young people and social media. In my opinion, comparison is a large part of the mental health issues many of our youth experience. Social media itself is often a breeding ground for comparison.

Now, let me be clear. I'm not against social media (and social media is not the only place we compare ourselves to others). But, I do recognize it makes comparison much easier. You may not even realize how it affects you if you haven't really studied how it makes you feel. I also recognize that social media can be good for some. We didn't have social media when I was young. However, I loved watching Ty Detmer play quarterback for BYU when I was a teenager. He had a profound impact on me. He was a great competitor, and his success at BYU 1989-1991 inspired me to chase my own dreams because I could see similarities between us, such as our height and hair color, and this fueled my drive to succeed. Seeing him on my social media feed probably would have motivated me as a kid!

This is a prime example of "ignition," a term from The Talent Code[1] by Daniel Coyle, which describes the energy and motivation which arises from witnessing someone else's success. When you see someone achieve their goals, it can light a fire within you to strive for your own accomplishments. However, the key to making social media a positive force in your life is to be mindful of your thoughts and reactions to others' success. If you find yourself inspired to dig deep and work harder towards your dreams, then social media can be an influence for good.

That said, a majority of the time, social media may leave us feeling worse about ourselves when we see the success of others. I would guess that around 80% of the time, when we finish scrolling, we feel less motivated than when we started. So when you open your favorite social media app, pay attention to how you feel after you close

---

1   (Coyle, 2009)

it. Are you comparing yourself to others? Do you feel as if you aren't doing enough? If so, maybe you should lessen your use.

As you become aware of your tendency to compare yourself to others when consuming social media, you also begin to understand when you need to take a break from it. If you find yourself constantly feeling worse or less empowered, it might be time to reevaluate your relationship with social media platforms. Afterall, the internet is a double-edged sword: never before has there been more negative and discouraging content available, but at the same time, there has never been more positive, empowering, and enlightened content. It's your responsibility to set boundaries, curate your algorithm, and decide what you consume.

If you're struggling, consider taking a break from social media for a week or a month. There will always be some version of social media in our lives, and we can't avoid it entirely. But, you can make it harder to access. Personally, Twitter can get me frustrated. So I took it off my phone. I can still access the site, and I'm still active on it, but I've made it harder to use because I have to sit down at my computer to login. This boundary helps me maintain distance from a platform which often discourages me.

Because comparison looms large in our current world—especially when it's time to compete or to build your career—I urge you to recognize the impact social media has on your life so it doesn't get in the way of your success.

Combatting Comparison

One of the most effective ways to combat comparison is to recognize that pressure and nerves are natural—even for the best of us—and to stay present in the moment. Feeling pressure and anxiety is not a sign that you are inadequate; on the contrary, it's an indicator you are on the right path and striving for more. There are people out there who seek jobs which provide only the bare necessities, and they purposely avoid pressure and challenges. However, the better part of us yearns for more, and with that desire, pressure and nerves become a natural and common occurrence.

Pressure is an indicator that you are pushing yourself to be better than you were yesterday. Stress and nerves are signs that you're on the right path because you are constantly learning and growing. Great achievers also feel pressure and anxiety, and they understand those feelings are not an indicator of results, but rather a sign that they genuinely care about their goals. Tom Brady once said, "I think sometimes in life the biggest challenges end up being the best things that happen in your life." That sentiment is shared by many successful individuals who see adversity as an opportunity to succeed.

Once you have accepted that pressure and nerves will be a part of your path, you can be more present in the moment and worry less about these feelings. The great ones understand the value of being present. When we focus on the present moment, and avoid comparing ourselves to others, we appreciate that pressure is a privilege and an essential part of our growth. By staying present, we transform our mindset and see challenges as opportunities, empowering ourselves to succeed and overcome the comparison trap.

Use W.I.N. to Stay Present

In sport psychology, we emphasize the importance of being present by using the phrase "Be Where Your Feet Are." This concept applies to both life and sport performance, as it's all about resetting your focus on the present moment. For example, a golfer needs to reset their focus approximately seventy-two times during a competition to consistently hit the ball straight. Similarly, a football player must refocus themself about seventy-five times during a game.

Peyton Manning once said, "In every football game, there are four or five plays that determine the outcome." What if you miss those plays because you are unfocused and in your own head? What if you don't miss those plays because you have mastered the art of focusing yourself? Since you don't know which plays will be the deciding factor, you have to stay dialed in on the present moment to perform at your best. This is true, not only for sports, but for life. Even Acceptance Commitment Therapy (ACT) points to presence in one's life as one of the largest factors of our own happiness.

One helpful tool to stay in the moment is the acronym W.I.N., which stands for "What's Important Now?" By consistently asking yourself this question, you can reset your focus, regardless of whether something good or bad has happened. The answer to "What's Important Now?" brings you back to the present moment and guides you toward positive actions that will benefit your current situation.

As performance coaches, we often talk about W.I.N. to help athletes get back to the present moment as soon as possible. The more we can avoid time-traveling into the future or the past, the better we'll perform. Some athletes I've worked with have even written "W.I.N." on their gloves, shoes, or chin straps to remind themselves of the importance of focusing on the present moment.

When adversity comes your way—and it will—it can be easy to fall into the trap of comparison. But, by standing tall and asking yourself "What's Important Now?", you'll be more equipped to maintain a positive mindset and keep your head in the game. When you make a mistake, in your life, in the game, or otherwise, don't dwell on that mistake. Accept that it happened and remember W.I.N. so you can focus on the next best action.

1% Better Rule

We often hear about the importance of self-improvement, but how do we actually make progress each day? James Clear, a well-known author, has introduced a powerful concept called the "1% Better Rule."

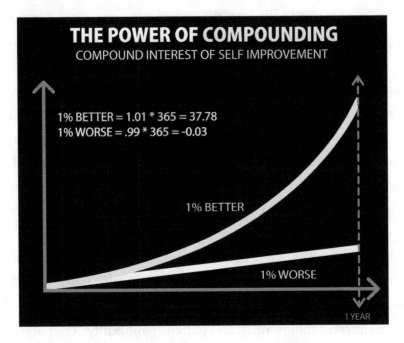

THE POWER OF COMPOUNDING
COMPOUND INTEREST OF SELF IMPROVEMENT

1% BETTER = 1.01 * 365 = 37.78
1% WORSE = .99 * 365 = -0.03

1% BETTER

1% WORSE

1 YEAR

This rule is a concept he discusses extensively in his bestselling book "Atomic Habits.[2]" The idea is simple but powerful: if you can

2   (Clear, 2018)

get 1% better each day for a year, you'll end up thirty-seven times better by the time you're done. Conversely, if you get 1% worse each day for one year, you'll decline nearly down to zero. This concept is based on the idea of compound interest, typically associated with money and investing. Much like how your wealth can grow through compound interest, your knowledge, skills, habits, and overall personal development can compound over time as well.

Steve Young, a professional football player for the NFL, spoke about this rule, and said, "The principle is competing against yourself. It's about self-improvement, about being better than you were the day before."[3] He couldn't have said it better. This rule is geared towards continuous improvement with the only person you should compare yourself against. You!

Improvement often creates happiness. By focusing on just one thing each day and getting a little bit better at it, we can experience the joy of growth. Small actions every day lead to impressive results. But they have to be the *right* small actions. Tom Brady said, "Most people are average because they work hard on things that don't matter." And if that's the case, what would happen if you focused on things that *do* matter and made it your entire focus each day? How far do you think you could go in your profession, your athletic ability, and your life?

In sport psychology, there's a concept called "negativity bias," where we tend to focus on negative outcomes, even when we've had a successful day. Meaning you could have worked hard to improve several different things today, and gotten significantly better at five of those things, but you would likely only focus on the two things you

---

3   (Young, n.d.)

didn't do better. And at the end of the day, as you are driving home or cooking a meal, these two things might consume your thoughts. This is negativity bias. Our minds like to linger on the things that didn't go well, versus the things which did. Even if we had a great day by most people's standards!

To combat this bias, we need to intentionally focus on one specific area of improvement each day and recognize our achievement when we improve. I truly believe we give power to what we focus on. To fight against this bias, we need to focus on one achievable goal each day. At the end of the day, take inventory—you either got better, or you didn't—and pick the next goal to focus on tomorrow.

In sport psychology, we call this "deliberate practice" or "intentionality." By choosing one aspect to work on daily, we can make significant progress. This approach simplifies the growth process, allowing us to clearly see whether we've improved or not. It eliminates the distractions which occur when trying to juggle multiple goals at once. And these goals don't need to be big. One day you can work on positive self-talk, the next you can work on the placement of your hand on a ball. You can change what you work on each day. Which is why the 1% Better Rule can help you in all aspects of life.

CHALLENGE 1

In this challenge, focus on overcoming comparison by embracing authenticity. Pick one of these things to work on each day this week and make a journal entry about how you felt at the end of the week.

1. Embrace your true self and understand that you are enough. The most successful and inspiring individuals are those who are genuine and unafraid to be vulnerable.

2. Offer sincere congratulations to those you admire. Genuine compliments not only uplift others but also have a positive impact on your own well-being.

3. Reflect on the positive aspects of your life and write what you are grateful for. This exercise will help you cultivate a more optimistic mindset and focus on what truly matters.

4. Don't wait for the perfect moment to take action. Seize opportunities as they arise, and make deliberate choices to move forward. Taking action with purpose will help you overcome comparison and build self-confidence.

CHALLENGE 2

Try reducing your social media and see how it makes you feel. Record your thoughts and emotions while using social media versus your thoughts and emotions after an extended period without using social media. If you can, try going one week without social media and record how you feel. This will help you become aware of how consuming this media affects your emotional wellbeing.

CHALLENGE 3

This is the Stop, Start, and Sustain challenge, and it is helpful to your performance, your mindset, and to your resilience. There is likely something in your heart right now you know you need to stop doing. So stop. And there is likely something in your mind telling you to start doing something. So start. Listen to your inner voice and trust it. Identify what you're doing that is good as well and pat yourself on the back for it.

Ask yourself these three questions to identify your Stop, Start, and Sustain.

1. What could I start doing today to be better at my craft?
2. What could I stop doing today to be better at my craft?
3. What could I keep doing today to be better at my craft?

CHAPTER 5

PERFECTIONISM

Every athlete strives to be the best at their chosen sport. And if you have experienced this need to be the best, it's likely this same determination and drive have helped you achieve impressive results. But, there is a darker side to your pursuit of excellence.

Perfectionism commonly gets labeled as competitiveness, and we might even claim ourselves to be "super competitive." But in truth, deeper down, this competitiveness is likely becoming an unhealthy quest for the unattainable—perfection. At the beginning of your sports journey, your perfectionism might have been a driving force that led to high performance. However, over time, it can lead to an overwhelming amount of self-criticism or negative self-talk, which are counterproductive and harmful.

To illustrate this, I often paint a picture for my clients where I have them imagine they are out on a boat with me enjoying a day of fishing on their favorite lake. Suddenly, we see a massive storm approaching on the horizon. The wind picks up, and the water starts to get choppy. To steady the boat, we decide to drop the anchor. But, in a perfectionist's mind, one anchor isn't enough. Instead, they drop eight anchors, believing that more will ensure safety. So we drop all eight of our anchors to hold the boat down, and the storm passes (never actually hitting us) but now we have another problem: The boat is taking on water because of the excessive number of anchors we've dropped. In an attempt to protect ourselves, we overcompensated and created more problems.

We do this to ourselves quite often. In order to protect ourselves from failure or disappointment, we overcompensate. We worry about things we don't need to worry about, and we imagine frustrating scenarios until we drive ourselves mad with the possibilities. And on top of all this, we often run into perfectionism's ugly twin sister whose name is negative self-talk.

In this same anchor scenario, a person who struggles with perfectionism might say to themselves, "I'm an idiot for dropping so many anchors," or "Maybe I don't belong on this lake because of my mistakes." These thoughts quickly spiral out of control and double the pain we are causing ourselves. We might even worry that the people we care about are disappointed in us.

Perfectionism, when kept in check, can be a powerful motivator. But when it spirals out of control, it leads to destructive thoughts and self-sabotage. The challenge is to recognize the difference and find a healthy balance in our pursuit of excellence.

Perfection Is Not Required to Win

Have you heard of Jim Thorpe? There is a photo where you can see him wearing different socks and shoes, and believe it or not, this wasn't a fashion statement.

Jim Thorpe was a Native American from Oklahoma who represented the United States in track and field at the 1912 Olympics.

On the morning of his competitions, someone stole his shoes. Instead of giving up or panicking, Jim managed to find two mismatched shoes in a garbage bin. One of the shoes was too big, so he had to wear an extra sock. Despite these challenges, he went on to win two gold medals wearing those shoes.

The moral of the story? He didn't let these challenges stop him.

He could have gotten in his own head and convinced himself others didn't want him there, so perhaps he didn't belong. But instead, he rose above and continued to perform in less than ideal conditions. This type of mental strength takes time to cultivate, but it will serve you in the long run.

Perfection is not required to win. It never has been.

Conditions don't have to be perfect for you to be successful. You can win when things are not ideal. It's essential to fight against perfectionism and find a way to make the best of whatever situation you find yourself in. Imagine if Jim Thorpe had let his circumstances get the better of him. He might have never realized his full potential.

In mental performance, we often talk about the 78% rule. This rule states that you can compete, scrap, and win even when you don't feel 100%. Think about your cell phone, when it is at 78%, does it give you full capacity and function? What about 53% or 29%? The answer is yes. Typically our phone doesn't start acting funny until we dip below 5%. That's a good time to recharge and recalibrate anyway. The point is this: you can still perform when you don't feel perfect.

No one is perfect. There is only one person who was. If you want to check your own imperfection, try filling a bathtub with two or three inches of water and place your foot in. If you hit porcelain, you're not perfect. Many of us, including myself, struggle with perfectionism. As a recovering perfectionist and a natural people-pleaser, I've learned the importance of giving myself grace and acknowledging I am doing the best I can with the tools I have.

To be one of the great ones, you need to accept that perfection is not the goal.

Negative Self-Talk

Negative self-talk has been scientifically proven to have detrimental effects on our mental health and overall well-being. In a large-scale study conducted by Kinderman et al. (2013)[1], it was found that self-blame and rumination can lead to mental health problems, including depression and a decreased ability to recognize and capitalize on opportunities. Furthermore, negative self-talk has been shown to significantly impact motivation.

Not only does negative self-talk fail to provide any benefits, but it can also become a self-fulfilling prophecy. On the other hand, positive self-talk has been identified as a great predictor of success. For instance, Walter et al. (2019)[2] conducted a study on junior sub-elite athletes and discovered that positive self-talk effectively reduced competitive anxiety and increased self-efficacy and performance.

Additionally, a comprehensive analysis by Tod et al. (2011)[3] examined the consequences of four distinct self-talk categories (instructional, motivational, positive, and negative). The researchers determined that positive self-talk was the most influential factor in predicting success. The study's findings indicate that instead of continually instructing themselves on how to perform a task, individuals benefit more from affirming their accomplishments and recognizing their hard work is acknowledged by others.

Yet even knowing all the science, perfectionism still creeps up on us. Our negative self-talk can lead to shame in both ourselves and our abilities. Research has demonstrated that shame is strongly linked to addiction, depression, and aggression, while guilt is associated with empathy and understanding other perspectives. The harsh reality is that shame thrives in the dark, hidden corners of our lives. It flourishes in secrecy and makes us feel isolated, as if nobody cares to listen.

Brené Brown said that the difference between guilt and shame is that shame states, "I am a mistake." Guilt states, "I made a mistake."[4] When put into this context, guilt can be motivational, and shame is most certainly demotivational. Because negative self-talk is the darker side of perfectionism, with all its shame and guilt, every high performer needs tools to identify and combat it.

Clues You Are Falling into Perfectionism

Some common signs of negative self-talk include the use of phrases like "I can't," "I don't," "I never," and "I always." These can indicate that you're falling into the trap of perfectionism. Here are some more clues that you might be struggling with perfectionism:

1. You "catastrophize" or engage in all-or-nothing thinking.
2. You have persistent thoughts of not being good enough.
3. You spend excessive time trying to achieve goals.
4. You find it difficult to relax.
5. It takes you a long time to finish tasks.
6. You often procrastinate.
7. Your self-worth is based on outcomes.
8. You frequently compare yourself to others.

4   (Brown, 2022)

9. Your standards for yourself differ from those you have for others.
10. Your self-criticism and self-talk are damaging.

Recognizing these signs can help you become aware of your perfectionist tendencies and work towards developing a healthier mindset. If you find yourself commonly doing any of the above, you are likely a perfectionist. Don't worry, I am too. I call myself a "recovering perfectionist" on the regular.

As I mentioned before, perfectionism can motivate you, but you have to walk a fine line between motivation and negativity. It is possible to walk away from negative self-talk. And when you do, you'll feel less stressed and have the ability to truly enjoy your life in its current state. Here are a few ways to combat the negative self-talk that comes with perfectionism.

Combating Negative Self-Talk

Negative self-talk shows up in many ways. It happens when we put ourselves down and don't believe in ourselves. This is commonly referred to as "imposter syndrome," and it happens to all of us.

Imagine you've just been promoted, landed your dream job, been given a leadership position, or won the starting position. What now? If your first thought is, "I hope nobody realizes I'm not good at this," you're not alone. My own uncle Bob frequently jokes about how he purposely keeps his high-powered, high-profile attorney job for only five years before everyone discovers he doesn't know what he's doing. Then, he moves on to the next department, firm, or opportunity and starts fresh. If you've ever told yourself, "I'm a fraud," "It's just luck," or "I'm just waiting for people to find out I'm in the wrong ballpark," you might be experiencing imposter syndrome.

If someone hands you a ticket for a rocketship to Mars, you get on and find out. At that point, there is no need to tell anyone why you aren't qualified. This form of negative self-talk, along with other forms, often happens when we feel exposed. It comes when we are trying something for the first time, and it comes when we make a mistake. Either way, it perpetually invades our mind.

In my own personal life as a sport psychology consultant, I feel exposed all the time! My podcast exposes me. This book makes me feel exposed. I am constantly worried that my colleagues will listen to my podcast or read this book and poke holes in my theories and thoughts and judge my anecdotes. I constantly fear that I am not well read enough, not experienced enough, and that I don't have enough training. Nonetheless, I constantly remind myself that launching my podcast was primarily driven by the desire to stay sharp, to invest time and effort, and to continuously improve. And writing this book has been yet another endeavor to hone my skills and refine my craft. Perhaps I can even make a difference in someone's life!

So how do we say goodbye to this negativity? It starts with flexibility.

Be Flexible

In nature, water exemplifies patience and adaptability as it flows seamlessly along its course. Rivers wind and adjust to the landscape, never fighting against their surroundings. Instead, they meander, twist, and turn, following the path of least resistance.

Your self-talk should mirror the fluidity of water, allowing you to seek solutions without forcing anything. Focus on growth, progress, and the journey, rather than overanalyzing every moment. Your goals will not happen overnight. When you are willing to take the long path, you'll find your progress will feel more natural and less stressed. As an example, when water is forced into an unnatural state, problems arise, such as broken dams or devastating floods. Similarly, it can be devastating for you if you force something you are not yet capable of. Flexibility in our self-talk and mindset helps us navigate life's challenges at our own pace.

A surprising example of flexibility is found in paper clips. Do you know how many paper clips were sold last year? Thirty-eight billion! That's five paper clips for every person in this world. Yet, how many paper clips do you think were used for their original purpose of pairing two pieces of paper together? My guess is less than 10%. So what do people use paper clips for? Replacing sim cards and zippers, picking locks, making key chains, clearing their salt and pepper shakers, and many other things I'm sure I don't even realize. Do you think the manufacturers go around complaining people don't use them for their intended purpose? No! Instead, they are happy to have created something which has a unique role for each of us.

Flexibility allows for the natural course of events to take place. Even if those events are different from what we expected to happen they often turn out better than we had planned.

When I was younger, I had an opportunity to string rackets for Utah State University's tennis team, where my dad was the head coach. I once witnessed a great player on the team, Rob Markosian, run out of rackets during a tournament. His serves were explosive, and so too was his temperament. But he was a unique player who I enjoyed being around, and he strung his rackets at a high tension, causing many of his strings to break when he played.

We were at one particular PCAA tournament in Ojai, California, and he broke another string on his racket, leaving him without a racket to use. I simply couldn't string his rackets fast enough! As I rushed to the court to let him know that I had not finished his other rackets, he yelled at me saying, "Bring me a f****** 2X4, I don't care, I can finish this guy off with anything you bring me!" So I did. I borrowed a less than desirable racket from another teammate. It wasn't pretty. But he won. He winked at me after the tournament and said, "I told you."

Rob didn't let the need to be perfect slow him down. Instead, he plowed headfirst into the game, unphased by circumstances that would have made other players stumble. He was flexible. Are you so inadequate at your sport, profession, or passion that everything must be perfect for you to succeed? The answer is no!

Perfection is not a requirement for success. You don't need the perfect equipment, weather, or circumstances. All you need is yourself. Whatever you woke up with this morning is enough. You are enough. Life will come at you fast, and it is not always fair. You can have excuses, or you can have results. But you can't have both.

Body Language

Body language plays a significant role in our self-talk and perception of ourselves. Most of us can agree that as we engage in positive self-talk, it often translates to improved posture and increased confidence. Interestingly, scientific research has shown that our body language can also influence our self-talk.

When I speak about body language, I often have the audience try an exercise. I ask them to stand in a slouch stance with their chins down and try to say a positive affirmation like, "I'm great at what I do." It's hard to do, and it feels very disjointed, because in this position, it's unnatural. Then, in the same slouched position, I have them say, "I suck." This is much more powerful and resonates deeply because their body language matches the words.

Next we switch to positive body language. A study from Amy Cuddy, a researcher and professor at Harvard, claims that when you peacock, or get bigger, it releases testosterone into your system. Though this study has had some pushback from peers, my own execution of this experiment seems to be working well for my clients. We do this through the power pose. The power pose resembles a Superman or Wonder Woman stance, with feet shoulder-width apart, hands on hips, chest out, shoulders back, and chin up. In this position, repeating the same affirmations yields similar results but reversed. Now, saying, "I suck" feels strange and disjointed, while the statement "I'm great at what I do" feels powerful and genuine.

The power of the way you stand has an influence on the way you feel about the words you say. When you stand in this pose, with your chin up, making yourself bigger with your arms, you can shape your thinking into something more helpful. Adopting a power pose can release positive hormones like dopamine, serotonin, and oxytocin, which contribute to happiness and contentment.

It may surprise you to learn that an astounding 80% of our communication is nonverbal. Consider the last time you played a game and noticed your opponent had thrown in the towel. How did you know? Chances are good their body language gave it away. This is precisely why it is crucial for us to be aware of the messages we are sending with our own posture, gestures, and expressions, both on the field or court and off. Even if you don't think you are in sales, you are. You are constantly selling to your boss, your coach, your teammates, your opponents, your family members, and your fans.

Our body language acts as a "billboard" for others and our own internal mind. By consciously adopting powerful poses and positive nonverbal cues, we can actually influence our own thoughts and emotions in an uplifting way. These thoughts have a direct impact on our performance.

Red Light, Yellow Light, Green Light

The late Ken Ravizza's "red light, yellow light, green light" thinking is a useful mental framework to understand our thought patterns and how they affect our performance.

To visualize this concept, imagine a board with red light thinking on the left, yellow light thinking in the middle, and green light thinking on the right. Red light thinking often includes persistent negative thoughts, imposter syndrome, and self-doubt. It's normal to experience these thoughts; as we know, 77% of our thoughts tend to lean towards negativity according to the negativity bias. This is where imposter syndrome activates and we think, "I don't belong here. I can't. I'm not as skilled as I need to be."

On the opposite side of the board is green light thinking, which is positive and empowering. When we are in green light thinking, we have thoughts of "I got this" and "I'm prepared." It's when we are in "flow" and feel good about ourselves. And, it's the mindset we strive for when we want to perform at our best. However, making the leap from red to green can be challenging, especially for elite athletes during high-pressure situations. It can be an enormous jump from red to green. We put a tremendous amount of pressure on ourselves to think positively, even in negative situations. This is where yellow light thinking comes in.

When we are struggling, it's hard to accept positivity from others or even ourselves. Yellow light thinking allows us to distance ourselves from the negativity and move closer to a positive mindset. Instead of trying to force the jump from red to green, the goal is to shift into a *neutral* state of mind; it's similar to taking a time-out for your mindset. Getting to neutral is a whole new world of thought that can improve performance. Transitioning from red to yellow is a more manageable step, and once we're on neutral ground, we can regain control of our spiraling thoughts. But how do we get to neutral?

3-2-1 Breathe

This is my favorite tool for getting to neutral. This tool, which I call 3-2-1 Breathe, is a grounding technique adapted from psychology. It brings you back to the present moment by focusing on your senses.

I have a friend by the name of Justin Su'a, who is a sport psychology consultant and mental performance coach for the Tampa Bay Rays, and he often talks about an experience he had while playing baseball at sixteen. While in an epic battle between his team and their opponents, Justin was experiencing an off day. Nothing he did was going right, from the way he pitched to the way he thought. Everything that day was wrong. And admittedly, his emotions were getting the best of him.

His frustration noticeable, his father, the coach, called a time-out and came out into the field. Usually as a coach his father knew what advice to offer so that he could tweak something small and perform better, but that day he said, "Are you hungry?" At that moment, Justin was confused. The question was off topic and didn't have to do with the nail biting game they were currently playing. But he nodded and said, "Kind of."

His father nodded and proceeded to take Justin's order. He said, "What do you want to eat?"

Justin said, "A burger."

His father asked "What kind?"

And Justin said, "A burger, with cheese, and a soda."

His father nodded, then proceeded to give Justin his own order of a double burger with cheese, extra onions, and a soda. Then he turned around and walked off the mound ending the time-out! He only called a time-out for that conversation. Weird, right?

Except it wasn't. Justin's father was tactfully giving Justin a time-out mentally and helping him reach a more neutral state of mind. As his father smiled at him from the sidelines, Justin realized he felt at ease. It was his fathers way of telling him, "Relax, you've got this." Because of this interaction with his father, Justin ended up turning it around, and his team won the game. All because his father helped Justin pause, taking his mind out of the game and off the things that were causing him stress.

This grounding technique can do the same for you. It involves focusing on three things you can see, two things you can hear, and one thing you can feel (physically, not emotionally), followed by a deep diaphragmatic breath. Focusing on your senses gives you a thirty-second break from reality and the barrage of negative thoughts that can overwhelm you. Some athletes I work with want even more space and do 3-3-3 Breathe, which is three things they can see, three things they can hear, and three things they can touch.

The 3-2-1 Breathe technique can be incredibly powerful in high-stress situations because when you give yourself a mental time-out, focus on neutral things, and shift your mindset, you can function at a higher level, with more clarity. With this tactic, you achieve yellow light thinking. The next part of yellow light thinking is productive thinking. This means simplifying our thought process to focus on one or two productive things that can help us in the present moment.

Ask yourself, what advice would you give to a young athlete in your shoes to be successful? Or how would you help your best friend if they were in the exact same situation you're facing right now? These are the thoughts you should concentrate on when engaging in productive thinking. Narrow your focus to one or two things that you know will improve your results and block out everything else. Imagine guiding someone you care about through the same scenario you're in. Be honest, acknowledge the situation, and concentrate on one or two controllable factors at that moment.

Reaching a neutral or productive state is crucial because we often overanalyze sports and situations in our lives. Today, sport is analyzed down to a science. To execute a perfect golf shot or for a quarterback to throw a football accurately, hundreds of factors come into play. But, it's not possible for us to consider every aspect needed to achieve the perfect shot.

By simplifying and getting to productive and simple thoughts, you allow your mind to unlock and you let your body do the work.

You already know how to perform the task, having done it thousands of times, and this technique cuts the mental noise and lets your body take over.

Other Ways to Neutral

If the 3-2-1 Breathe technique isn't for you, I have one more.

At Westminster College, there was an athlete who shot free throws at a 37% rate, whereas a great free-throw percentage would be near 80%. His coach, at a loss, asked for my help to improve his performance. When I spoke with the player, I asked him what he was thinking while standing at the free-throw line. He expressed worries about letting his team down, disappointing his family, and being the reason his team wouldn't win.

So, I recommended he stop thinking about that, and think instead about a song. I asked him if there were any songs he knew every word to. He was a returned missionary and chose "As I Have Loved You" from the LDS hymnbook. By singing this song in his head, he pushed out negative thoughts and substituted in a neutral thought unrelated to the situation. Which in turn unlocked his body's ability to perform the task he already knew how to do. As a result, his free throw success rate increased to over 75% for the rest of the season!

The essence of yellow light thinking is to replace any negative or counterproductive thoughts. Once you become proficient in yellow light thinking, transitioning into green light thinking becomes easier. It enables you to take small, manageable steps towards a positive mindset, rather than attempting one giant leap.

Counterarguments

When trying to combat negative self-talk, think of it as if you are dodging a punch. Counterarguments punch back against the overwhelming thoughts that bring you down. And you should be punching as hard as you can against the negative thoughts in your head.

Not all of our thoughts are true. Just because they come in your voice, to your mind, doesn't mean they're accurate statements. Sometimes we have to push back and remind ourselves they aren't true. To do this, use the phrase "That's not necessarily true... (and add something that is true about your situation)."

One helpful technique is to have athletes make a list, during a non-emotional moment, of everything they are proud of accomplishing. When you write these down in a place that is easily accessible to you, you can refer back to that list in emotional moments. Now, these words are yours, they are true, and you can use them to remind yourself of your progress so far.

For example, if your negative thought is "I don't belong here," you can counter it by saying, "That's not necessarily true...I have a state record in track and field in this event."

This way, you can fight back against the negative thought with something that is true and linked to a positive accomplishment. Having this list prepared is a powerful tool to combat the negative thoughts that might slip into your mind.

Caboose Arguments

For the realists reading this book, there's another approach to counteract negative self-talk called "caboose arguments." Some people might find the phrase "that's not necessarily true" to be unconvincing or ineffective for them. Maybe it doesn't feel like it's authentic in nature. Caboose arguments offer an alternative that allows you to accept the negative event that is happening by putting the word "BUT" at the end of the sentence.

For example, if you're thinking, "I'm having a hard time today," you can add a caboose argument by saying, "I'm having a hard time today, but I have a state record in track and field in this event, and I know that the hard work of this workout will make me better."

This approach allows you to acknowledge the less-than-desirable situation you're experiencing. The "but" serves as the caboose to the negativity, shifting your focus to positive thinking and reinforcing your confidence and abilities.

"YET" in All Its Power

The great ones understand each moment is uniquely designed for your progress. You win or you learn, and failure is feedback. Those who have achieved greatness often have a desire to continue to grow, progress, compete, and learn. They understand that anything worthwhile takes a little bit longer and is a little bit more difficult than anticipated.

One tool the great ones use is the power of the word "yet." When you get a case of the "I can'ts" or the "I don'ts," focus on using the word "yet" to get you through the moment.

"I just can't shoot free throws." …yet.

"I just don't close the way she does." …yet.

"I can't finish the way the coach wants me to." …yet.

"I just don't compete well in the clutch." ….yet.

The power of using the word "yet" comes from the book "Mindset" by Dr. Carol Dweck, the director of neuropsychology at Stanford. And the reason the word "yet" is so powerful, is because it reminds us that our story is not yet written. We often think we are further along in our journey than we actually are, which can lead to feelings of inadequacy or disappointment. By adding "yet," we give ourselves more time to develop and grow.

It also allows us to metaphorically call a time-out and put more time on the clock. Some athletes have been known to say, "We didn't lose to those guys; we just ran out of time." I love that mindset!

Using "yet" is a great tool to combat negative self-talk that stems from perfectionism, which can be demotivating. It helps us recognize that there is still time for improvement and that our current situation doesn't define our entire story. We are constantly under construction, with the ability to construct our dreams the way we want them to be.

Reset Routines

Ken Ravizza, a Sport Psychology Consultant, employed a unique approach while working with the Fullerton State Titans baseball team. He added a baby's training toilet into the dugout, with the full sound of a flushing toilet, enabling players to flush away their mistakes... literally! By walking to the end of the dugout and flushing the toilet, they engaged in a visual and auditory process that signified the end of the event, allowing them to move forward.

There is a psychology in not only saying things to yourself to move on, but doing a physical action that *reminds* you to move on. These routines work because they combine physical actions with mental processes. Just as we raise our hand and swear on the Bible in court or engage in religious rituals that reinforce our beliefs, reset routines help us remember our promises and move on from setbacks.

Various reset routines help athletes in different sports. A college volleyball player I worked with would redo her scrunchy while repeating empowering words, reminding herself that she belongs on the court. In contrast, a college softball player I worked with would drink Gatorade from a paper cup and throw it away, symbolizing the elimination of the undesired result. A baseball player I worked with would undo their gloves then fasten them back up to reset. And remember our football player with the control circle on his wrist? As part of his reset routine, he would press the circle drawn on his wrist to act as a reset button, shifting his focus away from the bad event to the next play.

Reset routines are designed to help us give the play, the pitch, the swing, the shot, or whatever mistake happens, a life and death of its own. The event happened, it's over, and now it's time to move forward. By incorporating a reset routine into your mental toolkit, you can effectively break free from the grip of negativity and refocus your energy on the task at hand.

The power of a reset routine lies in its ability to provide a tangible, immediate means of shifting your mindset away from negativity and toward a more constructive, focused state of mind. By engaging in a reset routine, you give yourself the opportunity to start fresh, free from the weight of past mistakes, and concentrate on delivering your best performance in the present moment.

Please remember, it's completely normal to battle perfectionism. No matter who you are or how far you get in your career, it is likely something you will face.

CHALLENGE 1

Practice bravery today. Do something today that you feel uncomfortable doing. Ask for directions. Start a podcast. Have a crucial conversation with someone. Call a therapist and set an appointment. Apply for a job that is out of your league. Download a meditation app. Apologize to someone you've done wrong. Do it today. You've got everything to gain.

CHALLENGE 2

Practice a counterargument today:

Try saying this to yourself: *"I'm having a thought that (insert counterproductive thought), but that might not necessarily be true."*

As a second part of this challenge, try using a mindfulness app like HeadSpace or Calm in your daily routine. I have been using HeadSpace since 2016, and I feel it has made a significant impact. I have felt a noticeable boost in awareness, a lowering of anxiety, and an increase in focus.

CHALLENGE 3

Think about the last time your inner critic was getting after you. Think about the words you were saying to yourself. Now, think about yourself telling the person next to you as if they were you. Suddenly, it makes us feel uncomfortable. What you say to yourself is often not acceptable to say to others.

If you wouldn't say it to others, you shouldn't say it to yourself. Practice positive self-talk this week.

CHAPTER 6

UNREALISTIC EXPECTATIONS

When was the last time you didn't meet your own personal expectations? How did you feel?

Too often we have higher expectations of ourselves than what is possible. The extent to which we fail to meet our own expectations often correlates with our level of frustration or anger. These feelings only increase when we feel we didn't meet the expectations of others such as our parents, teammates, coworkers, bosses, coaches, and friends.

We need to level with ourselves and ask: What do we expect from our marriages, relationships, careers, and performance? And from those expectations, what are we *realistically* capable of?

When you are unrealistic in your personal expectations, you set yourself up for failure. No matter how much you achieve or how much progress you make, you still feel "behind." You never take a minute to stop and celebrate the success of your progress because you still haven't met the lofty expectations you have placed on your own shoulders.

When it comes to expectations, I often remember a quote by Socrates, the Greek philosopher: "What screws us up most in life is the picture we have in our head of how it is supposed to be." This idealized image of how our lives should look can get in our way if we let it. However, I would argue that the gap between this picture of our life and reality of our life is where our growth lies. Until we can let go of what we think we "should" be doing, happiness will remain elusive. In fact, no matter how successful you become, you'll always feel discontent if you cling to this notion of what you "should" be.

Once you let go of that image, you start winning.

Self-sabotage can take place if you don't enjoy the ride along the way. You didn't get this far just to get this far. You've got a long way to go, but you can also appreciate how far you've come.

Don't "Should" All Over Yourself

The word "should" isn't meant to control your life. Failure is a part of striving towards success. You cannot have one without the other. So feeling as if you "should" be perfect, or you "should" have reached a certain level only creates toxicity for yourself. Failure is often fertilizer, not poison, for our lives. Yet it is treated like poison.

Theodore Roosevelt delivered a speech in 1910, often referred to as "The Man in the Arena." In this speech, he said, "It is not the critic who counts; not the man who points out how the strong man stumbles, or where the doer of deeds could have done them better. The credit belongs to the man who is actually in the arena, whose face is marred by dust and sweat and blood; who strives valiantly; who errs, who comes short again and again, because there is no effort without error and shortcoming; but who does actually strive to do the deeds; who knows great enthusiasms, the great devotions; who spends himself in a worthy cause; who at the best knows in the end the triumph of high achievement, and who, at the worst, if he fails, at least fails while daring greatly, so that his place shall never be with those cold and timid souls who neither know victory nor defeat."[1]

Often, the critic mentioned in this speech is not external, but internal. We are our own worst critic, and our mind constantly makes us feel as if we should do better. But just like Theodore Roosevelt said in the above, what matters is the *effort*. Failure is good; it is progress, and "should" has no place in that progress. It only takes away from the endeavor of effort and dredges up feelings of inadequacy. Your inner critic doesn't count. Be a great teammate to yourself.

This idea also connects to the Acceptance Commitment Therapy (ACT) we mentioned previously. Unrealistic expectations of ourselves and our lives create feelings of depression and dissatisfaction. ACT is highly focused on teaching participants how to accept things as they are, so you can then make adjustments in your life with a realistic understanding of your current situation.

Not understanding your current situation, and having unrealistic expectations of yourself, often leads to unrealistic time frames. If we don't have a clear picture of our current situation, and have lofty goals we want to achieve, we might think we can complete said goal in a year even though this very goal will likely take several years to complete. Then we are disappointed in ourselves when the year passes by and we still haven't achieved our goals.

It's because of this, in the field of sport psychology, we often joke that people with unrealistic expectations, perfectionism, and comparison tendencies set themselves up for punishment, almost like mental masochists. Especially because expectations often create

---

1   (Roosevelt, 1910)

more problems than they solve. Holding the unrealistic view that it is not okay to make mistakes can significantly impact the decisions and risks you're willing to take for success. You end up blocking your own path with your ideas on how things "should" be.

We frequently tell ourselves things like "I should already be the captain of the team," or "I should have placed first in that race." It's not bad to have high expectations for yourself, but it's the unrealistic time frames that often lead to "shoulding" all over yourself.

Here are some examples of "shoulding" all over yourself:
1. "I should be perfect in school." Nobody is perfect.
2. "The world should be fair." Not realistic, as many things are beyond our control.
3. "My golden years should be golden." Challenging to achieve due to the numerous transitions in life.
4. "My marriage should be easy." You get the point.

So stop "shoulding" all over yourself. There is nothing wrong with dreaming big. You are meant to dream. But your expectations should be centered around what you are realistically capable of doing.

Toxic Criticism

I have friends who tell me they don't care what others think. And truly, I find that hard to believe. I find myself wanting to ask, "Is that true? Do you *really not* take interest in what others think?"

That might be great in theory, but most of us do care about the opinions of others. When we hear criticisms, too often we see them as truthful. In fact, we often believe they are *more* truthful than what we know is true in our own minds, which only inflames our unrealistic expectations of ourselves and makes us feel like we "should" be better at something than we are. In our minds, we think maybe if we achieve the next level of greatness, the negativity will stop.

Sadly, this isn't the truth.

We assume success will automatically bring love and admiration from others, but over the past several years, I have worked with high profile athletes who have achieved the "success" many dream of and they still deal with toxic criticism. I am often shocked at the ferocity of fans and observers. The darkside of being a famous and successful athlete is often darker than you can imagine.

My colleagues and I have become increasingly alarmed by the vicious, malicious, and humiliating comments directed at athletes. It's hard to fathom how their parents and loved ones cope with this constant barrage of criticism. High-profile college and professional athletes face mounting pressure, and this has taken a toll on their mental health. Since March 2022, there have been five NCAA athlete suicide deaths. Athletes, with their still-maturing brains, are expected to make mature decisions under immense stress and scrutiny. And on top of this pressure, social media has significantly altered the landscape of sports, often with devastating effects on athletes' mental well-being due to how easy it is for spectators to make their negativity known to the player.

So how do we tackle toxic criticism?

First, remember Theodore Roosevelt's speech—it's not the critic who counts. It is you and your progress that count. Dealing with toxic criticism on a personal level can be challenging, but with the right mindset and strategies, you can protect your mental well-being and stay focused on your goals. Here are some practical ways to handle toxic criticism and maintain a healthy outlook on life. Remember, if you wouldn't seek someone out for advice, why would you give any weight to their criticism?

1. Seek support from loved ones. Share your experiences with friends and family members who can empathize and offer encouragement. Regular conversations with people who care about you can help alleviate the emotional burden of toxic criticism.

2. Recognize you are not alone. By acknowledging toxic criticism is a widespread issue, you can gain perspective and build resilience. Joining support groups or engaging in open discussions about toxic criticism can foster a sense of camaraderie and help you feel less isolated.

3. Limit exposure to negativity. Actively manage your interactions with potentially harmful sources of criticism. This could mean taking a break from social media, adjusting your privacy settings, or muting notifications from certain individuals. By controlling your environment, you can reduce the impact of toxic criticism on your mental health.

4. Reframe the situation. When faced with toxic criticism, try to view it through a different lens. Consider the source of the negativity and question their motives or credibility. For example, if an online troll is criticizing your work, think of them as an insignificant distraction rather than a valid judge of your abilities. This shift in perspective can help you maintain confidence and motivation.

5. Practice self-compassion. Remind yourself that nobody is perfect and it's okay to make mistakes. Instead of internalizing

toxic criticism, treat yourself with kindness and understanding. Focus on your achievements and progress, and celebrate your successes, no matter how small they may seem.

6. Advocate for change. By raising awareness of the harmful effects of toxic criticism, you can contribute to a more positive and empathetic culture. Share your experiences, promote kindness, and support others who are facing similar challenges. By standing up against negativity, you can help create a more compassionate and supportive environment for everyone.

Tools for Unrealistic Expectations

You'll be surprised to know a little gratitude goes a long way to destroy any unrealistic expectations you may have. A female golfer named Taitum Beck who I work with demonstrated the power of gratitude through her mental game log. She created a checklist covering various aspects of her performance, such as pre-performance routines, emotional control, and breathing techniques. At the end of each log entry, she included a gratitude journal section where she listed three things she was grateful for that day and one thing she had learned.

By reflecting on her achievements and focusing on areas for improvement, she maintained a positive mindset, even when faced with failure or mistakes. This approach allowed her to continuously grow and develop as an athlete, while also nurturing her mental resilience. I know it might sound surprisingly simple, but studies have repeatedly shown the benefits of gratitude.

Gratitude

A 2014 study published in Emotion magazine discovered gratitude can significantly improve our relationships. And according to a 2012 study in Personality and Individual Differences, people who are grateful tend to prioritize their health and take better care of themselves. But that's not all! Research by Dr. Robert A. Emmons has confirmed that cultivating gratitude can increase happiness and reduce depression. A 2012 study from the University of Kentucky found those who scored high on gratitude scales were better at coping with stress and adversity. And a 2006 study in Behavior Research and Therapy found Vietnam War veterans with PTSD experienced higher resilience when they practiced gratitude.[2]

With all this science to back it up, it's hard to ignore the benefits of gratitude. Cultivating gratitude doesn't cost us any money. Cultivating gratitude doesn't take much time. Research shows that the benefits of gratitude are enormous. Gratitude can also enhance performance. Wanna be clutch? Be grateful.

Gratitude even affects our sleep. A 2011 study in Applied Psychology: Health and Well-Being revealed simply jotting down things you're grateful for can lead to better and longer sleep. In a world and a competitive field where every second counts, and every percentage point changes results, these findings are not just significant: they are epic.

---

2   (Morin, 2015)

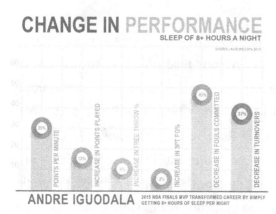

CHANGE IN PERFORMANCE
SLEEP OF 8+ HOURS A NIGHT

SOURCE: JAWBONE DATA 2015

POINTS PER MINUTE — 29%
INCREASE IN POINTS PLAYED — 17%
INCREASE IN FREE THROW % — 1%
INCREASE IN 3PT FG% — 2%
DECREASE IN FOULS COMMITTED — 45%
DECREASE IN TURNOVERS — 37%

ANDRE IGUODALA 2015 NBA FINALS MVP TRANSFORMED CAREER BY SIMPLY GETTING 8+ HOURS OF SLEEP PER NIGHT

Cheri D. Mah, of Stanford University, has been studying athletes for the last fifteen years and she has some incredible findings. In one portion of her study, basketball players for the Stanford Cardinal improved their speed by 5%, their free throw percentage by 9%, their three-point field goal percentage by 9.2%, by simply increasing their team average of sleep from 6.6 hours to 8.1 hours per night over two months. In another portion of her study, after obtaining extra sleep, Stanford swimmers swam a fifteen-meter sprint 0.15 seconds faster, reacted 0.15 seconds faster off the blocks, improved turn time by 0.1 seconds, and increased kick strokes by five kicks.

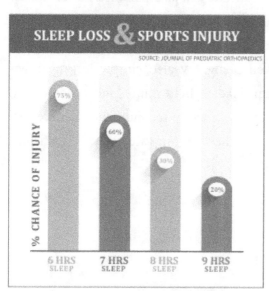

SLEEP LOSS & SPORTS INJURY

SOURCE: JOURNAL OF PAEDIATRIC ORTHOPAEDICS

% CHANCE OF INJURY

6 HRS SLEEP — 75%
7 HRS SLEEP — 60%
8 HRS SLEEP — 30%
9 HRS SLEEP — 20%

Crazy, right? A focus on gratitude not only grounds you and helps you fight against unrealistic expectations, but it also improves your sleep so you can perform better. Who wouldn't want that? With gratitude you can combat "shoulds" and toxic criticism because you are constantly reminded of what you've accomplished so far. It's a highly effective and underrated tool everyone can take advantage of.

Other Tools for Your Back Pocket

Here are some additional tools you can use to combat unrealistic expectations and bring more balance and positivity into your life. Try out a few and see which ones work best for you:

1. Use humor. One way to defeat unrealistic expectations is to find the humor in them. You could say things like, "That was a funny one," "Check out this grandiose expectation," or "That's a pretty interesting evaluation of our situation." Sometimes, simply acknowledging how hard you can be on yourself can put things into perspective.

2. Employ the double standard technique. Ask yourself, "What would I say to a loved one in this situation?" This can help you see how you may be treating yourself more harshly than you would treat someone else.

3. Reflect on the impact of your expectations. Make a list of the consequences or results of your unrealistic thinking. Reviewing how this thinking negatively impacts your life can show you that these expectations may not be helpful.

4. Practice compassion and forgiveness for yourself. Remind yourself that it's okay to make mistakes and that you're doing great things. Keep working on improving today, tomorrow, and whenever you can. Forgiving yourself out loud can be extremely beneficial. "It's okay, Riley. You're doing the best you can with the tools you have."

5. Allow for flexibility. Be open to change, as change is just change—it doesn't have to be bad. Embrace different approaches as they may offer valuable insights and opportunities for growth.

Dreams Don't Produce

Dreams are good to have. Don't think with all this talk of unrealistic expectations you should not have dreams. But, the truth is, dreams alone won't get you far. Progression requires more than dreams; progression requires a plan.

There are significant differences between dreams and plans, and understanding them is key to achieving success:

- Dreams exist in your mind, while plans require action. Your plans are the practical steps you take to turn your dreams into reality.
- Dreams can go on forever, but plans have specific time requirements. Effective plans are focused and detailed.
- Dreams come without cost, while plans demand time, effort, work, and sometimes even money.
- Dreams don't produce results, but plans do. Plans move you physically, mentally, and emotionally from point A to point B.
- Dreams are well, dreamy, whereas plans are grounded in reality. Plans keep you rooted in the practical steps you need to take.
- Dreams can motivate, but plans change your life and habits. While everyone has dreams, few people execute them on a daily basis.
- Dreams expand your imagination, but plans stretch you. Plans increase your abilities and skills and leave a lasting mark on your future.

So, let your dreams inspire you, but remember it is your plans that will truly make the difference. Take a look at your dreams, scrutinize them closely, and ask yourself: What is my plan? Do I have specific plans each day that can help me get closer to my dream? And are they realistic? Your dreams can work for you if you view them as flexible plans and not simply expectations.

CHALLENGE 1

Create a gratitude journal. Every night before bed, jot down three things you're grateful for. Keep it concise; it can be as brief as "1. Car, 2. Job, 3. Scholarship." If you're feeling inspired, expand on each item with a sentence or two. And if you're truly enthusiastic, choose one of the three and write to your heart's content.

Maintaining a Gratitude Journal not only nourishes your mind but also serves as a powerful reminder of the positivity in your life when you look back on your entries. This practice is an excellent way to counter the "negativity bias" discussed earlier in this book and helps you focus on the aspects of your life that uplift and support you.

CHALLENGE 2

Take a moment today and write a letter to express your gratitude to someone who has made a positive impact on your life. In our fast-paced world, taking the time to acknowledge and appreciate the wonderful people around us can be easily overlooked. Your message doesn't need to be lengthy; just a couple of paragraphs will suffice. But, by writing this letter, you'll not only lift their spirits but also lift your own.

PART 3

MOTIVATIONAL ALLIES

Have you ever watched "The Rookie"? In my opinion, this movie is a timeless classic. It's a great cinematic experience and an enlightening study in sport psychology.

It's based on a true story and features Dennis Quaid, who plays Jim Morris, a high school baseball coach, who had given up on his dream of playing in the major leagues. Throughout the movie, he is challenged by his high school team to try out again, and he ends up quitting his job to pursue his dream. As he does, he finds himself continually doubting his potential and wonders if he even has what it takes to get where he wants to go. It's at this pivotal moment when he confesses his struggles to his wife that we get a pivotal moment for Jim. She simply asks him, "Do you still love it?"

This question echoes in Morris's mind as he watches a news segment about his audacious decision to quit his job and chase his long-lost dreams. The news story serves as a lens through which we the audience see the montage of the many people who've supported Morris on his journey. It showcases his wife, his supportive high school baseball team, and even a pair of elderly gentlemen from his hometown of Big Lake, Texas, who believed in him. The entire time he holds this simple question in his mind, "Do you love it?" And then the sight of a young boy passionately playing baseball, smiling and waving at him, awakens something within. The love for the game, the memories of his supportive community, and the realization of his own capabilities. He remembers that he *does* love the game, and it's a passion which carries him into the major leagues.

So I'll ask you: do you love what you do? Even if you feel like you aren't performing 100% at it, do you still love it? Because we won't always perform at 100% in any aspect of our lives.

Jim Morris defies the odds in "The Rookie," but he didn't do so without doubt plaguing him along the way. He pulled himself out of these thoughts and fought for his dream which seemed out of sight, but unfortunately many don't. Usually, because they don't know how. This is where the Self-Determination Theory (SDT) can help you.

SDT is a comprehensive theory exploring human motivation and personality. It examines both intrinsic and extrinsic motivations and the roles they have to play in cognitive development. Based on the findings within SDT, there are three parts of the theory which help consistently improve an athlete's mental health and motivation:

1. Autonomy (I call it "I choose")
2. Competence (I call it "I can")
3. Support Network (I call it "I belong")

These three things—autonomy, competence, and support network—are the building blocks of Self-Determination Theory. Whether you are an athlete, a business owner, or a stay at home parent, these three blocks will help you stay motivated and confident even when the world around you becomes difficult to navigate.

In the upcoming sections, we will delve deeper into these three allies so you can use them to boost your confidence and motivation and to serve as a preventive measure against burnout. I focus on these three pillars because they form the basis of what I call the "Self-Confidence Theory," and I teach this theory to my clients with a focus on "I can," "I choose," and "I belong." These three motivation allies are tried and true scientific practices. If you *choose* to be somewhere, and you know you *can* do a task, and you know you *belong* where you are, confidence and motivation come naturally.

CHAPTER 7

AUTONOMY—I CHOOSE

According to a quote attributed to Ralph Waldo Emerson, "The only person you are destined to become is the person you decide to be."

The image of an ideal life can hold us back if we let it. Your life needs to be true to your needs and desires. If you are performing based on what others want you to do, or going a specific direction because your parents or loved ones say it would be better, you won't be as committed to your path. When you haven't chosen what you do, and adversity comes your way, perseverance is almost impossible. Until we can let go of what we think we "should" be doing, we won't find happiness.

In fact, no matter how successful you become, you'll always feel discontent if you cling to this notion of what you "should" be. It is only once you let go of that image you can start winning.

Mark Twain said, "The two most important days in your life are the day you are born and the day you find out why."[1] Autonomy is where you find out the "why" of your existence. It is the agency

---

1   you find out why."

of choosing your own path. When you have agency in what you are doing, you typically have more grit, resilience, and moxie, because you *chose* it. Your parents didn't make the decision. You did.

No one typically feels motivated when others make decisions for them. Can you remember a time when someone took a choice away from you? Maybe it happened when you were a toddler. Maybe it's happened much more recently within your adult life. Did you get angry? Did you want to give up? Did you feel resentful towards the person who took your choice away? If you said yes to any of these, that's normal! Look at the world around you. It's easy to see, in politics, worldwide conflicts, and relationships, that people get angry when their autonomy is removed by others.

But surprisingly often, the main person removing our autonomy from us is ourselves.

Instead of pursuing what we love, we "should" all over ourselves and push ourselves into boxes we think we belong in. And I get it! Choosing your own path can be tough. Self-doubt is rampant. Your mind plagues you with the question, "Is this the right choice?" And we wonder so often about if we are right or not, we often forget the golden question.

Do you love it?

If you are good at football, but you love baseball, it doesn't mean you *have* to pursue football. It is not required of you. We put up so many barriers if we aren't inherently good at something, thinking to ourselves that maybe we shouldn't do that thing. But you'll be surprised at the solutions you find, and the changes you make, once you start down the path of something you love. To do something impactful, it's got to be your choice, otherwise you will likely quit.

Remember when you were a kid and you discovered what you loved? It could have been a sport, activity, instrument, or something else. But none of us will ever forget how it felt to be a kid and discover that we really *loved* something. Play for that kid inside of you who fell in love.

Autonomy Shapes Our Lives

What do you think is the biggest factor when it comes to happiness? Money? Good looks? Power? Popularity? While these things definitely don't hurt our pursuit of happiness, there is something which more powerfully influences our overall satisfaction. According to a report by the Journal of Personality and Social Psychology[2], the top influencer of happiness is actually autonomy. When the activities and habits in your life are chosen and endorsed by you, you are happier.

A key to happiness and success is your ability to choose your own path and feel in control of your life. This is backed up by a University of Michigan survey[3], which reported that 15% of Americans who felt they were in control of their lives also reported feelings of happiness. So, ask yourself: Are you currently doing things you don't want to do? Are you stuck in a job where you lack autonomy and control? Are you just going through the motions each day, feeling like you don't have a say in what you do?

If you answered yes to any of these questions, it's time to take a hard look at your choices. Maybe some of your habits or daily routines are holding you back. Maybe you feel as if you don't have a choice in some of the things you do. You'll be surprised to hear how making small changes in your life which allow you to exercise more control can make a big difference.

Yale psychologist Judith Rodin encouraged depressed nursing-home patients to exert more control in their lives by motivating them to make a few small but key changes in their environments. For example, Rodin made sure patients were asked to decide for themselves if—in their room—they wanted the air conditioning on or off, if they'd like to change the channels on the TV, if they'd like to have different foods for dinner, or if they'd like to rearrange the furniture in their rooms. Rodin even pushed patients to request changes in various nursing home policies. As a result, 93% of these patients became more alert, active, and happy. Again, this theory was tested in prisoners who were allowed to move chairs and take control over lights and TV remotes. Once more, they found the happiness of the prisoners increased.

You can start taking more control in your own life with small steps. Identify a task you need to do today, write it down, and cross it off once it's done. The simple act of completing tasks and checking them off a list can amplify your confidence and prepare you to tackle other challenges. Next, begin choosing exciting projects or events, mark them on your calendar, and make sure you make them a priority. Even if you go alone. Even if no one else is interested in these projects or events. The important thing is that *you* picked them, and you are doing them only for you. Another effective strategy is learning to say "no." Start saying no more often because every no gives you the opportunity to say "yes" to something more important or meaningful. Occasionally, saying no could be the key to restoring balance to your life.

Commitment Over Motivation

According to Howard Hunter, the 14th President of the Church of Jesus Christ of Latter-day Saints, "True greatness requires consistent, small, and sometimes ordinary steps over a long period of time." The path to greatness is often lined with what some might call the "lonely work." It's about falling in love with the mundane, the monotonous, and the repetitive. There is a unique enthusiasm the great ones possess for these ordinary tasks. They understand there is no substitute for patient, continual hard work.

But you have to choose this work. Consistency is a key ingredient for growth, which hinges on commitment. To be consistent, you need to be committed, and to be committed, you need the autonomy to make the choice to commit.

I personally believe that commitment carries more weight than motivation. Would you prefer your significant other to say they are motivated to marry you or committed to marrying you? Most people would choose commitment because commitment carries a sense of permanence and determination that motivation lacks. If my wife is motivated to be married to me, it's a state that could easily waver. However, if she's committed, it's not something she'll give up on easily.

Yet, people chase motivation, as if it will be the golden solution to their problems. They want to feel the drive and the passion *before* they put in the work. They feel if they are not motivated to do something, they shouldn't do it at all. But, the great ones, those who find great amounts of success in whatever they pursue, understand commitment supersedes motivation. They don't need to "feel" it to take action. And they understand motivation comes and goes, but commitment is what keeps you showing up, even when the motivation has long since disappeared.

But what is commitment? I've heard athletes say, "I want it, so I'm committed to it." But just wanting something isn't good enough. Sure you said "I choose" to take this action, you exercised your autonomy, but you also have to be diligent in doing everything you can to get the results you want.

Commitment Is More Than a Choice

There is a story I commonly share with my clients to demonstrate commitment in full swing. It starts with a young man who has ambitions to work for a high paying prestigious company. It was the golden goose of employment opportunities. Armed with a polished résumé and an unwavering resolve, he navigated through a series of interviews and finally landed an entry-level job. But that wasn't enough. The young man was highly motivated to move up within the company and had his eye on the next prize—a supervisor position that promised greater prestige and a fatter paycheck. With this goal in mind, he threw himself into his work. He arrived early, stayed late, and made sure the boss was well aware of his long hours.

Five years of this routine passed, and finally, a supervisor position opened up, and the young man applied. However, he wasn't chosen for the promotion; instead, it had been given to a colleague who had been with the company for a mere six months! Filled with anger, he stormed into his boss's office, demanding an explanation.

The boss, a man of wisdom, looked at the young man and said, "Before I answer your questions, would you do me a favor?"

"Sure," responded the young man, still seething.

"Would you go to the store and buy some oranges? My wife needs them."

Despite his frustration, the young man complied. Upon his return, the boss asked, "What kind of oranges did you buy?"

"I don't know," the young man answered, confused. "You just said to buy oranges. So, I bought oranges."

"And how much did they cost?" the boss probed.

"Well, I'm not sure," was the flustered reply. "You gave me $30. Here is your receipt and your change."

The boss thanked him and asked him to sit down and pay close attention. He then summoned the newly-promoted employee and asked him to do the same task.

When the employee returned, the boss asked, "What kind of oranges did you buy?"

"Well," he began thoughtfully, "the store had many varieties— navel oranges, Valencia oranges, blood oranges, tangerines, and more. I didn't know which kind to buy. But then I remembered the oranges were for your wife, so I called her. She mentioned she was hosting a party and planning to make orange juice. So, I asked the grocer which oranges would make the best juice. He recommended the Valencia oranges. I bought those and dropped them at your house on my way back."

"And the cost?" the boss asked.

"That was another dilemma. I wasn't sure how many to buy, so I called your wife again. She was expecting twenty guests. I asked the grocer how many oranges would be needed for twenty people—it was quite a lot. I managed to negotiate a discount for the large quantity. Normally, the oranges are seventy-five cents each, but I got them for fifty cents. Here's your receipt and the change." The boss smiled, thanked him, and dismissed him.

Talk about a difference! Both their efforts differed, as did their attention to detail. However, I would argue that the most profound distinction was not in the task itself, but in their level of commitment to the task. The employee who received the supervisor position demonstrates that it takes more than simply choosing to do something. It takes a high level of commitment to see it through to the best of your ability.

Autonomy within the Self-Determination Theory directly relates to the level of commitment in your heart. Sometimes simply choosing to do something isn't enough. You have to be deeply committed to the choice. Romantics use the phrase, "Choose your love, and then love your choice." Though they are likely speaking to relationships, I think you can apply it to your other commitments as well. Choose your plan, and then love your plan.

Upping Your Commitment

How can you move beyond just "choosing"? Here are some key strategies to consider to reinforce your commitment.

1. **Be Mindful of Over-Analysis:** A key stumbling block many encounter is overthinking or over-analyzing their goals, which often leads to indecision paralysis. Remember, commitment and indecision cannot coexist. It's important to strike a balance between careful consideration and taking decisive action.

2. **Cultivate Self-Awareness:** A fundamental element of deepening your commitment lies in understanding your own strengths and weaknesses. This process involves being able to confront your flaws without self-defeat, acknowledging them, and devising an improvement plan. When you sincerely commit to this personal

growth plan, you'll begin to attract supportive individuals who can help strengthen your resolve.

3. **Write Down Your Commitments:** The simple act of writing down your commitment can be an immensely powerful strategy. There's a unique clarity and force in translating your intentions from mind to paper. This not only compels us to thoroughly think through our decisions but also to articulate them with precision.

4. **Share Your Commitment with Trusted Individuals:** It can be incredibly beneficial to share your commitment with a select group of friends or family members who you trust. However, be cautious in choosing these individuals, ensuring they truly have your best interests at heart. Sharing your intentions with a supportive group allows for regular check-ins and encouragement, strengthening your commitment.

5. **Cultivate a Caring Attitude:** An often overlooked aspect of commitment is caring—for others, their goals, their aspirations, and their own commitments. Seek out mentoring opportunities. Guiding others along their path not only allows you to help them but also bolsters your ability to care for yourself. This reciprocal care amplifies your own commitment and makes it easier to stay the course.

Be Authentic

Authenticity is fundamental to our autonomy and, consequently, our ability to make meaningful choices. Authentic people are often the happiest, most balanced, and ultimately, the most successful. They are genuine, trustworthy, and consistently inspiring to those around them. And because they know exactly who they are, they make choices which resonate with things they love.

My grandfather, Clark Owen Thompson, was a World War II veteran from the greatest generation. He wasn't a decorated soldier, a celebrated entrepreneur, or a millionaire whose wealth trickled down generations. But, he was a legend in our family. He loved his wife dearly, he loved his children dearly, and he did many things in his life. He was a certified mortician, he served a mission for his church, he owned his own grocery store, he sold wigs and insurance, he even sold carpet! By the standards of his day, he wasn't the most successful business man ever. However, every choice he made, and every path he took, he loved. He was a hilarious hard worker who was happy with himself and didn't mind wearing many hats.

He lived his life authentically. His values could be seen on his sleeve, and he encouraged all of his children to find their authentic selves. He was so loved, that today, over ten of his great-grandchildren bear his names, Clark or Owen, a testament to the lasting impact he had on our family.

Authenticity unlocks our maximum potential. It paves the way for growth, progress, and a fulfilling life because we understand who we are at our core. Becoming more authentic means becoming true to yourself. If you need help doing this, so you better understand what choices are right for you, here are five steps that can help:

1. Redefine Your Values: What principles guide your actions? Discover them and live them passionately.
2. Foster an Open Mind: Embrace the diverse world around you. We live in an age of abundant information. Use it to broaden

your perspective by reading insightful books, listening to thought-provoking podcasts, and striving to embody the good you seek.

3. Practice Vulnerability: Fill in the blank: "If you really knew me, you'd know this: _____." Sharing personal truths can be daunting, but it fosters authenticity and deepens connections.

4. Acknowledge Inauthentic Moments: When you deviate from your values, recognize it. Living in alignment with your principles brings joy and fulfillment.

5. Trust Your Intuition: Your gut instinct is a powerful guide. Whether it's a gut feeling, a heart tug, or a spiritual nudge, trust it. Your intuition is there for a reason—to lead you towards promising opportunities.

Remember the E+R=O formula? The space between the E (Event) and the R (Response) is where our power lies. It's where we get to make our choices. Embracing authenticity not only strengthens our self-trust but also boosts our confidence. It's about making the conscious choice to uphold our values, to trust our intuition, and to engage with the world as our most genuine selves. And this newfound confidence encourages us to seize beneficial opportunities that improve our lives, our families, and our communities.

CHALLENGE 1:

Pick two things this week you *want* to do and give yourself a healthy deadline. Make sure the tasks are something you can reasonably do within your set deadline. Then go and do them! You will feel better and more in control of your life when you do this.

CHALLENGE 2:

Start committing. It might seem unusual at first, but begin nurturing the habit of aligning your words with your actions. And make sure those actions are completed to the best of your ability. Remember the orange story and don't just "choose" to do something, choose to do everything within your power to make sure the task is completed more than others would expect. Feel the difference and begin applying this in your choices moving forward.

CHAPTER 8

COMPETENCE—I CAN

Competence is a way of utilizing and interpreting our past experiences to predict future results. Now, don't get it twisted—competence and confidence, while related, are distinctly different.

Confidence ebbs and flows; it's a feeling. It's the wind beneath our wings one day and the cold gust that knocks us off balance the next. On the other hand, competence is a steady companion. It's our past victories, lessons learned, and skills honed over time. These experiences help us understand what we are capable of.

If you ever sit across from me in one of my sessions, I'll ask you to compile a list which catalogs accomplishments and moments in your life you are proud of. I mentioned this in Chapter 5 when explaining counterarguments. This list then becomes your personal arsenal, a handy tool for those moments when adversity attempts to knock you down. It's a written testament to your resilience and a physical reminder of your past victories that screams, "You've done this before. You can do it again."

That is competence. Reminding yourself that you *have* done something difficult, and you *can* do it again.

In job interviews, when I've been asked, "Why should we hire you?" My answer has often been, "I believe that if you give me the right training, I'm smart enough and competent enough to be successful at what you ask me to do." At first glance, this might sound like confidence, but in reality, it isn't. It's a statement grounded in competence and born from past experiences and successes. It's a reminder to *myself* that given the right circumstances, I can rise to the occasion again.

The path to success is often longer and more challenging than we anticipate, but this difficulty is often an integral part of the journey. The difficulty of the journey adds value to the destination. With competence in your corner, every step along that path, every stumble, every victory, builds a future brimming with possibility. Competence is not about a fleeting feeling—it's about knowing, deep down, that you've got what it takes to face whatever comes your way.

Competence Is a Mindset

Have you ever watched "Gattaca"? In the movie's not-too-distant future, advancements in biotechnology and eugenics have cleaved society into two groups— the "valids" and the "in-valids."

"Valids" are those born from manipulated embryonic genes, chosen to inherit their parents' most superior genetic traits. On the flip side, "in-valids" are conceived naturally and subjected to the luck of genetic draw. Because of this, they are often considered flawed. They're more prone to genetic disorders and weaknesses, barred from esteemed professions, and relegated to mundane work.

The protagonist, Vincent Freeman, is an in-valid, carrying genes predisposing him to various disorders, and he has an estimated life span of just over thirty years. Despite being stuck in a janitorial job, Vincent secretly aspires to be an astronaut, a career that his genetic profile disqualifies him from.

Anton, Vincent's brother, is a valid, which only heightens their sibling rivalry. In their childhood, they'd often engage in a game of "chicken," where they swam into the ocean until one of them would chicken out and turn back. Vincent, the underdog, would invariably lose, until one day, he left Anton, the genetically superior sibling, in his wake. Anton, exhausted and unable to keep up, nearly drowned, only to be saved by Vincent. Fast forward several years, a relentless and ambitious Vincent manages to infiltrate the space program and earns his place on a Saturn-bound mission based on his own merit. The brothers face off again in their childhood game, and once more, Vincent outpaces Anton, saving him from drowning yet again.

Baffled and beaten, Anton asks, "How are you doing this, Vincent? How have you done any of this?" To which Vincent responds, "You wanna know how I did it? This is how I did it, Anton. I never saved anything for the swim back."

Vincent, despite society's labels—too short, not smart enough, not the right genes—persisted. He embodied the essence of competence, channeling his past experiences, trials, and tribulations toward his dream. His mindset was not limited by his genetic profile or societal expectations; he understood what he was capable of and harnessed it, with an unshakeable belief in his ability to conquer the challenges before him. His competence, rooted in this mindset, proved more powerful than any artificially enhanced genetic superiority.

In sport psychology, there's a highly sought after state of being often referred to as the "zone." This is a state of perfect focus, where everything falls into place almost effortlessly. Being in the zone is something almost everyone has felt at one point in their life, but it is next to impossible to duplicate on demand.

Many have studied "being in the zone." Time slows down. It's an out-of-body experience. Things fit together naturally. We suddenly have a perfect shot, or a perfect catch, or maybe even a perfect business meeting. The few times I have been in the zone in my life, I remember dropping back to throw a football in the game, and when I threw it, everything slowed down, I was guiding the ball, and it went exactly where I needed it to go. And experiencing this perfect moment in time makes us want to try and find it again. But in all our studies, we have never found the formula to replicate this feeling or to trigger this experience.

In our search to duplicate these moments, numerous methods have been explored, such as pre-performance routines, controlled breathing, visualization, and imagery, all aiming to enable athletes to enter this zone at will. But in truth, while all of these methods are helpful, none of them truly allow us to duplicate the feeling of being in the zone on demand. We know what you need to do to get there and what it feels like to get there. But we haven't bridged the gap between the two.

So the current best answer is to rely on competence because it's a lot easier to get into the zone when you remind yourself you have been there before and you have found success within it. It's not about being the perfect athlete who needs their A game to win. Rather, it's about understanding that you are competent enough to win with your B, C, or even D game. You don't need to be the tallest, smartest, strongest, or fastest. Because throughout your life, you've proven that you can succeed without being the best in these categories, often by a significant margin. This is what the list helps us to remember.

Success doesn't require perfect conditions. Need to play a tennis match in the national championship, and you're faced with forty-mile-an-hour winds? Doesn't matter! Your focus should be on giving your best with the current circumstances. You don't always need to be in the zone to win. Leaning into your competence can carry you through.

When I reflect on my own journey, many people I meet seem to grapple with a discrepancy between their perception of greatness and their current abilities. During my time in football, I struggled with this. I wasn't always blessed with the strongest arm, I wasn't always the fastest quarterback, and I certainly wasn't the tallest. I may not have had the best accuracy or the most delicate touch. I was good or even great at many of these characteristics, but oftentimes not the very best on my team. Yet, what set me apart in the Division 1 football world was an unwavering commitment: I vowed that no one would outwork me, and no one would be better prepared.

Even with seemingly average abilities, it's possible to excel when you foster the right mindset. I wasn't bothered if someone could throw the ball farther than me; I knew I could throw far enough. Remember, the lion doesn't lose sleep over the fact that it's not as fleet-footed as a cheetah, as large as an elephant, as tall as the giraffe, or as agile as an antelope. Instead, it recognizes its own strengths and leverages them. And, despite lacking these qualities, it's the lion that reigns supreme.

Why? Mentality. The lion embodies courage and boldness. It strides with fearlessness, never looking back. It steadfastly believes in its prowess, is willing to take risks, and views any animal as potential prey. It perceives every opportunity as worth exploring and never allows one to slip away. A lion doesn't succeed at every hunt. We don't need to be the best to succeed. What we truly need is courage, the will to try, faith in the possibility of success, and belief in ourselves and our capabilities.

Find Your Strengths

If you know your strengths, you know your competencies.

Dennis Rodman and Kyle Korver are two notable figures who effectively leveraged their strengths to carve out successful careers in the NBA. Dennis Rodman, despite his struggles offensively with free throws and three-pointers, honed his skills in rebounding and tenacious defense. He realized his unique strength lay in these areas, and by concentrating his efforts on them, he built an impressive nineteen-year career in the NBA. Kyle Korver, while not exceptional at defense or rebounding, was remarkably gifted at sinking three-pointers and free throws during high-pressure moments. His shooting prowess not only secured his place in the NBA but sustained a remarkable seventeen-year career. They each understood their strengths and used them to their advantage!

Another who pays attention to his strengths is Tom Brady. He wasn't the most physically athletic quarterback, yet he's often touted as the best QB in NFL history. And he wasn't even drafted in the 1st round! Drafted in the sixth round, Brady focused on honing his strengths rather than improving areas that didn't have a significant impact on his performance. Imagine if Tom Brady spent an exorbitant amount of time trying to improve his forty-yard dash time? He would have been working on something that had no bearing on his ability to play amazing football at his position. This approach allowed him to flourish. Tom Brady is a lion.

Perhaps one of my favorite instances of understanding your strengths is Lionel Messi, a football (soccer) player known for his uncanny ability with his left foot. During one memorable match, Messi scored a goal with nineteen out of twenty-one touches made with his left foot. Though many critics mentioned he should stop using his left foot so often early in his career, focusing on this unique strength allowed Messi to emerge as one of the greatest footballers in history.

Marcus Buckingham, the author and business consultant, eloquently posted on Twitter about Messi's left foot. "Twenty-five years ago," he wrote, "I penned a book about what the world's best managers do differently. The key finding was this: they instinctively draw out what God left in, rather than put in what God left out." Buckingham encouraged us all to find our "left foot," that unique and powerful part of us that unlocks our potential and unleashes our awesomeness.

Messi understood his strength. He knew he was adept with his left foot, even when others didn't see it. Messi is a lion. He didn't focus too much on something else, or try not to use his left foot as his critics suggested, which might have taken away from the opportunities he's created for himself. And just like Messi's left foot, your unique strengths and competencies can guide you down a similar path to success.

First, you need to understand what your strengths are. Martin Seligman, a renowned positive psychologist, has developed a free online resource known as the Via Strengths Finder. This tool invites you to answer a series of questions, consequently providing an overview of your top twenty-four emotional and mental strengths.

You can find this enlightening assessment at ViaCharacter.org.

Once you've unearthed your strengths, you'll realize that you possess a depth of understanding and experience in these areas. In fact, people will often tell me they don't have many strengths. But then when they take this test, they are astounded at how competent they are in the strengths listed as their own. These strengths might be innate or natural gifts you've honed over time. Recognizing them can boost your sense of competence and give you strengths to lean on when times get difficult.

In my work with professional, elite, and Olympic athletes, I've observed that when hardship strikes, these athletes—the great ones—lean into their strengths rather than dwelling on their weaknesses. They go back to focusing on what got them where they are in the first place, not on what didn't get them there. Awareness is a critical factor in achieving this mindset and, in my view, an essential ingredient for success in life.

What are your strengths? The last time you ran into an obstacle, did you lean on them? How much did your strengths help you through the adversity? Being aware of your strengths allows you to competently navigate hard times, but if you don't know what you excel at, you may be left scrambling when times get tough.

This principle applies to our shortcomings as well. If you are unaware of a wart on your nose, for instance, you'd never think to apply a remedy. In other words, we need to have a clear understanding of our life's landscape, which is why mindfulness and meditation are so important. These techniques enhance self-awareness, helping us look inward and tune into our thoughts, feelings, and actions. Armed with this awareness, we're better equipped to make informed decisions.

Once my clients have completed the Via Strengths assessment, I often discuss with them both the "sunny side" and the "shadow side" of their strength. Every strength has both. For instance, one of my strengths is humor. When this is your forte, you don't need much guidance on how to lighten a room with a well-placed joke. However, the shadow side of humor emerges when adversity strikes and you find it challenging to be patient or forgiving with those who don't resort to humor to alleviate the strain. As someone who naturally employs humor to ease tensions, I had to learn not to judge or grow impatient with those who don't share this coping mechanism.

An additional shadow side to my humor strength also comes when others see my humor as a weakness. For example, during tough times in my sales career, my tendency to inject humor into tough situations led to judgments about my seriousness and commitment to the job. People felt I didn't take my situation seriously and thought everything was a big joke. Trust me, as a recovering perfectionist, I did take my situation seriously, but I always kept myself going with a bit of humor. Remember, if someone sees your strength as a weakness, it's likely a reflection of the observer's perspective of your shadow side, rather than a true flaw in your strength.

Are you ready for the next step? It's a brave one. It requires asking a trusted individual to identify your top three strengths and one weakness, as they perceive them. It's about being willing to see how others view your strengths and being willing to ask, "What is my blind spot?" This can be a challenging conversation to have, as it requires a great deal of courage to face potential criticisms. However, a clear understanding of our competencies empowers us to navigate life's difficulties more effectively.

Recognize your strengths daily. Build on them. Cultivate them. Water them. Fertilize them. It will make all the difference. Van Gogh didn't become Van Gogh by focusing on the small details of his paintings. In fact, he openly embraced the mess of his art, which is what made him authentic and unforgettable in the process. Your strengths can do the same for you.

Go First

The most effective way to build confidence is by stepping outside of your comfort zone. For parents seeking to instill bravery and courage in their children, this is the secret—stepping out of your comfort zone every single day. The "go first" concept might make you feel slightly uncomfortable, but this is exactly what makes it so valuable.

"Go first" takes me back to a lesson imparted by my younger brother KC, a successful businessman in the tire industry who is also a former college football player, a coach, and a devoted father and husband. I remember him sharing an anecdote about his approach to conferences and training. He makes a point to be the first in role plays, sales scenarios, presentations, and so forth. He always goes first, and he always notices the one who steps up first during the training sessions he oversees. Like my brother, I now volunteer to go first, and it has made a significant difference in my confidence in myself.

Why?

Discomfort spurs growth. Stepping up to go first instantly places you in an uncomfortable position, but this discomfort is crucial for building confidence. Each time we make ourselves uncomfortable, we create new neural pathways that foster creativity and enhance our efficiency for the desired task. It also stimulates dopamine release, the "happiness" chemical. Happy people are confident people, and confident people perform well. Thus, "go first" propels you to perform at a higher level.

Also, volunteering first for a task, training, or a role play allows for greater authenticity. Authenticity attracts people. While authenticity generally means being honest with yourself and others, I believe it has more to do with vulnerability and courage. When you go first, you set the tone. And that tone of courage and vulnerability is contagious for the rest of the group.

In essence, "go first" encourages you to get comfortable with discomfort, a fundamental confidence-building mechanism. The cycle of stepping up, gaining confidence from positive outcomes, and building competence for future tasks is empowering. And you can start this process by simply having the courage to do something first.

More Heart, Please!

Heart is commonly connected to courage. The term "courage" originates from the Latin word "cor," a root found in multiple languages referring to the heart—"corazón" in Spanish, "le coeur" in French, "cardiac" in medical terminology, among many others. Even in our language, the two are interwoven together. And it's well known that giving something more "heart" means having more courage and resilience. It's something we need to utilize more in our everyday actions.

I attended a conference in San Diego where sport psychology consultants from across the country congregated. We discussed various topics, including control, focus and concentration, visualization, self-talk, and pre-performance routines. All of these elements are intended to build confidence in athletes, businesses, and professionals alike. We study the books, listen to the talks, and strive to make a difference. However, a realization struck me during this particular conference.

Regardless of the depth of scientific discussions we engage in, the truth remains that our lives require more heart. Our relationships, jobs, hobbies, conversations—in essence, everything we do—need more heart. As a sport and performance psychology professional, I love discussing the mind, mental resilience, and mindset. Yet, I've come to understand that we all need to put more of our hearts into what we do. My career choice itself stems from a sense of calling. I view my job as sacred and entered this field hoping to positively impact people's lives. However, sometimes, I find myself overly focused on the mind, neglecting the heart's importance.

Incorporating more heart into our actions is a testament to our courage and competence. The courage it takes to expose your heart is a testament to your competence in managing emotional vulnerability and authenticity. It shows a higher level of understanding of not only your strengths but also your limitations. The goal is to continually display vulnerability and emotional intelligence and to inspire others to do the same.

CHALLENGE 1

Visit ViaCharacter.org and take the Via Strengths Finder assessment. The insights you gain from this exercise can serve as a powerful foundation upon which you build your resilience, enhance your confidence, and amplify your competence. Next, ask a few people you trust to name your top three strengths and one weakness in their eyes to gain a greater understanding of your blind spot and how others view you.

CHALLENGE 2

Write down twenty words or signature strengths that describe you. Freewrite. Be creative. Compliment yourself. Now narrow it down to your top three strengths. These three are your signature strengths. Now, spend the greater portion of today noticing these strengths and noticing core signature strengths in others. Who has similar strengths to you? Why? Who has strengths that differ from yours? Why? And finally, ask yourself how you can implement these strengths more in your own life?

CHALLENGE 3

Invest your heart in everything you do. Put your heart into the dinner you prepare tonight, into the next conversation you have. Express your love to someone—it could be a parent, a coach, a family member, or a co-worker. Show your heart, expose your heart. Notice others who openly express their heart daily. You will be surprised to find how much more deeply you experience the world when your heart is in on the task.

CHAPTER 9

SUPPORT NETWORK—I BELONG

To be successful in life, you need to surround yourself by the excited, the inspired, and the grateful.

Whether in sports, business, or personal life, having a robust support network is a critical factor. Remember Tiger Woods? As a sporting icon, his struggles, both personal and professional, were laid bare for all to see. It must have been one of the most difficult and embarrassing times of his life. But he didn't stay down. After going through this rough patch, he attempted a comeback, initially appearing with his head bowed low. However, something remarkable happened a couple of years later. Woods won again, and this time, he didn't just pump his fist in personal triumph, he exclaimed, "We did it!"

Notice his use of the word "we." He didn't say, "I did it." Even in his moment of triumph, he didn't put the win on his own shoulders. Because the "we" referred to his team. He likely had an amazing team behind him, from coaches to caddies to friends and family. And he knew that he couldn't have done it without them. Woods understood that the win wasn't his alone, it was a win for all of them. And just like Tiger, each one of us needs to build a team of people in our corner.

The presence of a support network not only aids in sustaining motivation but also gives you a balanced perspective on reality. Remember the story of the emperor with no clothes, where he walks around naked because his subjects were too afraid to tell him the truth? You don't want to surround yourself with "yes-men." You need individuals who can provide you with honest feedback and help you see the truth even when it's uncomfortable. Being receptive to constructive criticism is a mark of a true leader. If you surround yourself with people who only sing your praises, you might find yourself moving through life making unnecessary mistakes.

Surround Yourself with Support

When you sit with winners, the conversation is different. Winners are consistently looking to improve, trying to meet the next goal, and seeking advice. They do not settle, and they chase away negative thoughts because they know those thoughts only serve to hurt their success. This is not the norm. The conversations of winners are often fundamentally different from the rest. It was Bill Parcells, the New York Giants football coach, who said, "Losers assemble in small groups and complain. Winners assemble as a team and find ways to win."

Think about the last time you were around a winner. Maybe they are a top performer in your workplace? Maybe they competed against you in a competition? You can spot them because others consistently want to be like them. You might have even felt this pull yourself. They are the people we ask, "How did you do that?" or "What did you do differently?" as we try to figure out how they crushed goals that everyone else struggled to meet.

Sit next to them. Talk to them. Learn what they do and how you can do it too. A true winner, one of the great ones, won't push away the opportunity to help another succeed. So take that chance and look to them for advice. They have developed a growth mindset, and you can too.

Jon Gordon wrote a book called "The Energy Bus," and in it he talks about "energy vampires." These individuals drain the positivity and motivation from their surroundings. I call these individuals "locker room lawyers," and unfortunately, there are too many out there pleading their case to teammates, friends, parents, and co-workers. They cleverly place blame and they have all the answers. You'll hear them in locker rooms, offices, and even family gatherings, spinning tales of woe that shift responsibility away from themselves. These are the people you shouldn't sit with. And you should avoid being a "locker room lawyer" yourself.

Instead, find solutions. And find them among the winners.

Establishing a strong social support network isn't just a reactive strategy for when times get tough. It should be something you proactively work at. Doing so can significantly contribute to your success and well-being. Think about that same winner you had in mind before. Who have you seen around them? Who do they confide in or spend their time with? Likely, the people around them are winners as well.

Social support is worth the hype, and it's not just me that believes so. Scientific evidence strongly underscores the importance of social support, especially when overcoming adversities such as injuries or setbacks. Athletes surrounded by a caring circle of teammates or friends tend to recover faster from injuries. And the presence of a few go-to people who can provide emotional support, practical help, or sound advice can make a significant difference when you face adversity. These individuals offer more than just a helping hand; they provide perspective, hope, and encouragement, often illuminating the pathway forward when the situation seems bleak.

Research across various disciplines also consistently affirms the role of social support in success. A robust support system has been linked to improved mental and physical health, higher levels of motivation and perseverance, and a better ability to navigate stress. It's no surprise, then, that the most successful individuals often attribute a significant part of their success to the support they've received from their network. It's not just about having people around; it's about the quality of these relationships and the mutual support they provide.

My Mother

From my earliest memories, my mother has been an unwavering pillar of support in my life. Her innate understanding in the power of belief has been instrumental in sculpting my self-assurance. There are two memories which come to mind where she made the difference in how I reacted to a difficult situation.

The first occurred during my senior year as the starting quarterback at Utah State University. My football career came to an abrupt halt when I sustained a concussion in the sixth game of the season. In that crushing moment, as my NFL dreams crumbled, I dialed my parents' number, my heart heavy with disappointment.

I expected sympathy or advice from my mother, but her response took me by surprise. She was genuinely startled! "I am so surprised, Riley, I have no idea what to say." Then we cried together for the loss of my football career. Her ability to just listen, not repair, was everything I needed that crisp October night. Rather than offering platitudes, she gave me something far more valuable: space to grieve, to express my sorrow, and to begin healing. When I asked about her response later in life, she simply stated she believed so strongly in my potential to play in the NFL that my injury took her by surprise. The thought had never occurred to her that I might not have a professional career.

The second time she helped me was when my wife and I faced a challenging pregnancy. At twenty-five weeks, we received the devastating news that my wife had HELLP syndrome, an intensified form of pre-eclampsia. After a grueling thirty-six hours, and my wife fighting dire circumstances, our daughter Alexis was born prematurely, weighing only 1 lb 6 oz.

As we navigated the uncertainties of the neonatal intensive care unit (NICU), I witnessed the fragility of life and felt my strength waver. We were told Alexis would have to be in the NICU for quite a while, but after only sixty days in the NICU with Alexis surviving scares with heart valves, possible brain bleeds, sticky lungs, and watching others in the NICU lose their beautiful children, I was exhausted. Both my wife and I were at the end of our rope. That was when Alexis turned a bluish hue, and my wife immediately knew something was wrong.

The next morning, I held my tiny baby in a sitting position in a tiny isolette while doctors tested her blood, gave her a spinal tap, and poked and prodded my child with needles. It was terrifying. I was petrified. I didn't think I could do it. After the events of that day, I was exhausted and overwhelmed, and I confided to my mother how I felt. I expressed my doubts and fears and said, "I can't do this for another sixty days, Mom."

To my surprise, her response was not one of sympathy. Instead, she reminded me of my newfound role as the quarterback of Team Jensen. Then she encouraged me to focus on the present moment. She said, "Riley, you can and you will. But don't plan for sixty days. Just make it through tomorrow."

My mother isn't a mental performance coach, but she did know the power of staying in the present moment. I took her advice and took it day by day. She helped me get through the one hundred and thirteen days Alexis stayed in the NICU. But she didn't do it with empty promises. She never told me everything would be okay or that I shouldn't worry. Instead, she stood firmly in my corner, reminded me of my role in this family, and reminded me to not let my mind run away with fear. Little did I know at that time how this experience would shape my future as a mental performance coach and sport psychology consultant.

My mother's resolute belief and unwavering support have reinforced my self-confidence, resilience, and determination. Her profound insights into the necessity of a solid team have been a guiding force throughout my journey. And her ability to lend an ear, to simply be there when needed, to hold space for my doubts and fears without rushing to resolve them, has allowed me to navigate life's complexities with greater self-assuredness and conviction.

The impact of my mother's belief in me extends far beyond the specific moments I described. It has become an integral part of my mindset and approach to life. Sometimes people warn parents that their voice (or criticism) becomes their child's inner voice later in life. I was blessed with someone whose voice did become my inner voice, and it was filled with nothing but belief. To this day, my mother's belief in me remains unshaken. I can still hear her voice appear as my inner voice, "Riley, you can achieve that. You've always accomplished whatever you set your mind to." How wonderful is that?

I want you to strive to populate your world, your team, with individuals who mirror my mother's unwavering belief. I understand not everyone has a mother figure in their lives, but you can find a support network to stand in your corner, rooting for your success, even without parental support.

As I work with athletes and individuals seeking to enhance their performance, I emphasize the importance of cultivating a supportive network and surrounding oneself with individuals who genuinely believe in their abilities. I encourage them to seek social support from those who will listen without judgment, provide encouragement, and offer practical guidance when needed. Navigating the terrain of excellence is no simple task. Doing so alone is even harder. But a reliable support network becomes our compass and shelter during the storms of uncertainty.

Surrounding yourself with a team that believes in your potential and provides unwavering support is a gift that continues to give. The support system you build for yourself can be your beacon of hope during times of struggle and a source of celebration in times of victory. So don't overlook its importance as you seek to be more motivated and confident. There is a reason it stands as the third pillar within motivational allies. Without a support network, life's challenges can quickly pull you down and make a "locker room lawyer" out of you.

You Can Do More Together

Draft horses offer a wellspring of lessons on teamwork, collaboration, and the power of social support in shaping our capabilities. These majestic and large horses—like the Shire, Belgian, Clydesdale, and Percheron—have shaped human history with their ability to pull immense loads and move heavy objects.

While a single Shire horse can pull up to 8,000 pounds, the true strength lies in their ability to work together. Two Shire horses pulling in tandem can pull not twice, but three times as much weight, reaching an astonishing 24,000 pounds. But their strength doesn't end there! When these horses have trained and worked together for an extended period of time, they collaborate together, and their coordinated efforts can pull a remarkable 40,000 pounds!

But this takes time. They have to work together frequently so they know how to synchronize their movements and help each other maintain balance. This is what enables them to move loads that far exceed what they could handle individually. The fact that two draft horses can pull five times the weight of one draft horse is a testament to the power of teamwork!

Just as these horses require shared experiences and training to maximize their potential, you do too. You need to spend time with your team to know how to collaborate with them. And once you do know how to work together, you can amplify your abilities through this collaboration. Forging strong bonds equips us with the power of collective effort, and drives us toward achievements that dwarf the individual feats we might have completed alone. Draft horses epitomize the adage that no man is an island; we flourish when we work together, support one another, and revel in the communal strength we possess.

Teamwork is an essential part of life. When we have a strong network of support, we feel more confident in our abilities, take on greater challenges, and achieve extraordinary results. The draft horses teach us that by cultivating meaningful relationships and giving them time to grow, we can empower ourselves and others to reach new heights of achievement.

Don't Let Tech Get in Your Way

Since the iPhone's introduction in 2007, there has been a noticeable shift in the social dynamics of younger generations, specifically 8th, 10th, and 12th graders. Alarmingly, more and more young people are reporting feelings of isolation, often agreeing with statements like "I often feel left out of things" and "a lot of times I feel lonely." These sentiments have been on a steady incline since 2007, coinciding with the rise of smartphone usage.

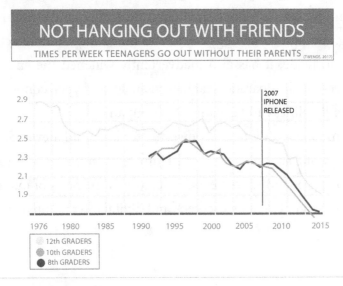

NOT HANGING OUT WITH FRIENDS

TIMES PER WEEK TEENAGERS GO OUT WITHOUT THEIR PARENTS (TWENGE, 2017)

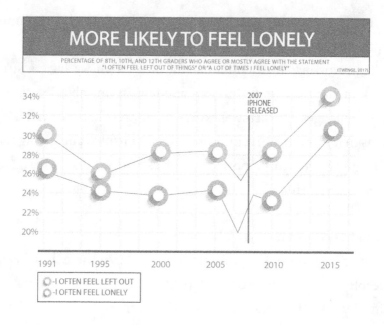

Moreover, the time teenagers spend with their friends each week has seen a significant decline in part because of technology. With the world at their fingertips, young people have increasingly replaced in-person interaction with virtual communication and social media browsing. Though technology does offer novel ways to connect with people worldwide, it has also inadvertently widened the emotional gap between us. It is paradoxical that in an age of hyper-connectivity, feelings of loneliness and isolation are rampant.

Technology, although a powerful tool, should never become a barrier in our support networks. Human connection, face-to-face communication, and shared experiences form the basis of our social fabric, and it's vital to not let screens and digital interactions diminish their value.

While technology has transformed the way we communicate, we need to strike a balance—embrace the advantages technology provides, but remain cognizant of its limitations and potential pitfalls. Make time for offline experiences, engage in real-life activities with friends, and ensure technology serves as a tool to enhance—not replace—your social interactions. A text or a "like" on social media will never replace the power and comfort of a smile, a laugh, or a heartfelt conversation. Building resilience, overcoming adversity, and enhancing mental toughness depends on strong, personal connections, not just strong WiFi signals.

The HOPE Experiment

Back in 1958, at Harvard University, Dr. Curt Richter pushed the envelope of the research of human potential when he started the HOPE experiment.[1] The goal of the study was to understand resilience and how it is affected by team support.

To measure this, Richter placed rats in a small pool of water with one job: keep swimming. On average, these gutsy rats managed to swim for about fifteen minutes before fatigue overcame them. But just as they started to sink, the researchers would swoop in and rescue these worn-out rats. They would act with compassion and offer the rats a chance to rest and recover. They would hug the rats and offer them gentle pats of reassurance. They did everything they could to make sure the rats were both physically and emotionally rested. Rejuvenated and instilled with a spark of hope, the rats were then put back into the water for another round of swimming. But this time, the outcome was drastically different.

---

1   (Richter, 1958)

These revitalized rodents, fueled by a newfound sense of hope and survival, didn't just keep afloat for another fifteen minutes. They keep going, defying all odds, for a jaw-dropping sixty hours of ceaseless endurance. You read that right, sixty hours!

When the rats believed in their potential rescue, they pushed their bodies to limits they hadn't even dreamed of reaching. Now, I want you to pause and think about that. If a mere dash of hope could trigger such incredible tenacity in these creatures, imagine what firm belief from your support network could do for you.

Think about the untapped potential lying dormant within you, just waiting for a dose of hope, encouragement, and a supportive word to bring it to life. Hope is the spark that lights the fire of possibility within all of us. Don't underestimate the power of a heartfelt compliment—it's like a high-protein breakfast for champions. A sense of belonging uncovers an infinite source of greatness. This is what the HOPE experience showed us, and this is what I want you to remember when building your support network.

Build Up Your Team

A support network is a two-way street. The great ones know they cannot only receive support, but they also need to offer support to those who help them. They don't just shower gratitude on their coaches and bosses. They understand that everyone plays a part, big or small, in their journey. Every role is pivotal, and every effort, no matter how minuscule, deserves recognition.

Herm Edwards, the former NFL player and coach, always talks about acknowledging the center, the unsung hero doing much of the hard work with minimal applause. When was the last time you acknowledged your own 'center,' the one who rolls up their sleeves, immerses in the dirty work, and takes a hit or two, just to ensure that you shine?

One person who has always lived by this principle is my mentor, Michael "Chico" Canales at NC State University. As a graduate assistant coach, I noticed early on that late into the evening Chico takes a moment to thank the custodians cleaning up after hours. But it wasn't just a simple thank you. He knew their names and the names of their children. I witnessed him thank these individuals by name, then ask them how their son enjoyed their birthday, or if their daughter was still in a barbie phase. He not only acknowledged them, but he *knew* them. Imagine being a custodian and having a major Division 1 coach not only notice you but genuinely care about you and your family. That, my friends, is powerful beyond measure.

Chico recognized and appreciated everyone who contributed to his journey. No matter how big or small.

John F. Kennedy loved the quote, "A rising tide lifts all boats." It's a timeless nugget of wisdom that many have echoed throughout the years. But have you ever stopped to ponder what constitutes the "rising tide"? And how do we go about creating it?

When I first saw JFK voice these words during his famous "Ask not what your country can do for you, but what you can do for your country" speech, I felt an alternative meaning stir within me. What if the "rising tide" he mentioned was a metaphor for kindness? Imagine if kindness towards your family, co-workers, teammates, and especially yourself could be the driving force for change.

In line with this, Bob Kerrey strikes a chord when he says, "Unexpected kindness is the most powerful, least costly, and most underrated agent of human change." Often, in conversations with athletes I work with, I emphasize to never underestimate the power of a well-timed, genuine, and authentic compliment or thank you.

As you build a support network, you need to build them up just as they build you up. To help raise the tide at your workplace, with your team, or within your family, here are a few tips:

1. Send or share a funny link with a teammate. Don't overthink it; just do it. Don't let the worry of whether they'll find it amusing or not bother them dampen your spirits. Remember, this exercise is as much about you practicing kindness as it is about them. Or better yet, send it my way! I love a good joke. Reach me at riley@rjpg.net.

2. In your next conversation, wear the interviewer's hat. Think of five questions you could ask your teammate the next time you see them. Be attentive—keep the focus on them. It's amazing what you can learn and the response you can elicit.

3. Invite a teammate for lunch or dinner. Choose someone you don't usually hang out with. This simple act can foster trust and benefit your team in unimaginable ways.

4. Pick up an extra hot chocolate/coffee/donuts for someone. Small gestures like these can make someone's day and may even set a trend within your team, and the circle of kindness will come back to you.

5. Pay genuine compliments to your teammates. Make them feel appreciated, as everyone should. Remember, compliments are

contagious. They reinforce the sense of belonging, and the stronger your team, the higher your personal success.

6. Write a heartfelt thank you letter to someone who impacted you. It helps people more than you realize.

I spoke with a highly respected coach—with a twenty year career—who was glowing when we talked because he had just received a letter from a former player. In the letter, he was thanked for the lessons and wisdom he passed onto the player. Now, believe it or not, this coach often felt like maybe his lessons were too over the top. But to get a letter saying those lessons had actually helped someone made him tear up! To me he said, "I'm sorry. I get so excited about these letters because I have only received three in my entire coaching career."

Only three letters is surprising, isn't it? Especially for someone who continually works to improve the lives of others and bring out greatness within them. Bear in mind, this isn't just any coach we're talking about. This is a mentor who has guided more than a hundred players onto the path of collegiate sports. A mentor who genuinely cares, maintains relationships, offers advice, and celebrates every victory with his players. He isn't a harsh, demanding coach. He is a coach who has made a significant impact on numerous lives. And he has only received three letters!

The impact you can make on your team simply by telling them the positive effect they have had on you is well worth the time. When was the last time you felt a surge of gratitude towards a coach? Or the last time you thanked your parents for their unwavering support?

These feelings of gratitude shouldn't be kept to ourselves; they should be shared. In doing so, we fortify our own team.

A true team isn't defined merely by the collective pursuit of a goal. Instead, it's shaped by the mutual recognition of each other's value and the equal cheering for each other's triumphs. When we express our gratitude, and we thank the unsung heroes in our lives, we are not only lifting their spirits, we're also reinforcing the foundations of our own support network.

In the grand tournament of life, each of us is both a player and a supporter. In this context, every letter of appreciation, every word of thanks, and every expression of gratitude contributes to a rising tide of mutual support and recognition. By acknowledging and appreciating each other, we ensure all our "boats" rise together.

Incredible individuals in our lives have cheered us on, supported us, and shaped us into who we are. They're out there, maybe even wondering if they've made a difference. Let them know when they have.

CHALLENGE 1

Take a moment to reflect on the individuals who have helped shape your life's path. Maybe it's a mentor, a coach, a family member, or a friend. Can you picture their face? Now, write them a letter. No, this isn't an essay assignment, nor a time for crafting perfect prose. It's a heart assignment, an opportunity to express genuine gratitude from the core of your being. All it takes is a few lines to communicate your appreciation. Once you've poured your thankfulness onto the page, pop that letter in the post. Old-fashioned snail mail might seem like a relic in our digital age, but trust me, the surprise of receiving a heartfelt letter will brighten their day in a way an email or text simply can't.

PART 4

GOING BEYOND MOTIVATION

Motivation is not always a good wingman. It comes and goes, and it isn't always there when you need it. Which is why you need strategies to continue when motivation is nowhere to be found. Especially because things are always new and exciting when you first start them, whether it be your job, a new workout, or learning a new craft, and motivation is commonly present during this time. But slowly, as you do these things more consistently, the newness ebbs away, and often, so does the motivation. This is why learning to love "the lonely work" is something that the great ones master early and often.

Now I know you might be shaking your head. Maybe thinking "I know successful people who are constantly motivated." But in reality, this isn't the case. Where you see motivation, it is likely instead a habit and a dedication to consistency. They have the knowledge of how to keep going even when their mind is screaming at them to stay under the blankets in bed. During the good and the bad, they have developed the mindset needed to keep going and know how to do so without burning themselves out. They don't label days as "good" or "bad." The days just are, and they make the best of them.

Whenever someone mentions the idea that any event in my life might be "good" or "bad," I often remember this story, and it might be one you've heard before. A father and son own a small plot of land, and together they dreamt of owning a stallion. Though they were poor and had no money to make their dream possible, they built a stable to accommodate a stallion anyway. Fortune seemed to smile on them because when they woke up one day, a stallion appeared on their land. It was the stallion of their dreams, and they gently caught it and claimed it as their own. The townsfolk were quick to celebrate their good luck, telling both the father and the son how lucky they were, but the father responded with, "Maybe you're right, maybe not."

But then, the stallion broke out, and the townspeople told them how unlucky that was. Again the father said, "Maybe you're right, maybe not." Then the stallion came back, bringing a whole herd of horses with him. Once again, as the townspeople congratulated them on their luck, the fathers only answer was "Maybe you're right, maybe not." As their story continues, they go through a series of fortunate and unfortunate circumstances, including the son breaking his leg and ultimately being spared from war because of his injury. But no matter what happened, each time the father responded with his enigmatic "Maybe you're right, maybe not."

In our fast-paced, snap judgment society, we are quick to label things as good or bad and believe these feelings are the truth of the matter. In this Google and McDonald's society full of quick and easy solutions, we think, "I don't feel like doing this thing today, so it must not be my dream." Or we might think, "I'm not doing well at this, so it must not be what I'm meant to do."

We label the hardships in our life as "good" or "bad" instead of just accepting them as roadblocks along the way and continuing along our path. Now, I acknowledge there are times to change the direction you want to move in, but it should not be a snap decision, and you cannot let a lack of motivation halt your progress.

My youngest brother, Crosby, is a great example of this story in a real life situation. He is currently a cognitive performance specialist for fighter pilots in the Air Force at Vance Air Force Base. I think his ability to teach mental toughness is directly related to this story. In 9th grade, at the end of basketball season, he took charge during the last game of the year. In doing so, he fell backwards and broke his left thumb. This was problematic for three reasons. First, try-outs for the high school varsity team were in two weeks; second, the high school team was also playing the next week in a large tournament; and third, Crosby is a left handed pitcher. Disastrous, right?

Maybe you're right, maybe not.

Crosby played at Cottonwood High School, a perennial baseball powerhouse in Utah. In hopes of playing as soon as possible, we went to Dr. Russ Toronto, a dedicated sports medicine doctor. He had Crosby bring his baseball bat to the office. They were able to construct a cast that was solely for his thumb and didn't extend past his wrist, and they formed his cast around the baseball bat so he would be able to grip the bat in competition. This also allowed him to grip the baseball as well as hit and throw the baseball with the cast on his hand. Crosby would be able to play as "pain permitted." What resulted was a great tournament with Crosby as a first baseman and hitter.

Crosby pushed forward even when he was in pain and unsure about his ability to perform. He didn't let a lack of motivation stop him. Instead, he put his mind to the task and found a way to perform at a top level even though his thumb was broken. Part of the reason he is so successful as a cognitive performance specialist for Air Force fighter pilots is because he was then and is now aware that motivation might not always be in your corner.

There is a book which is a must read called "Rules for a Knight" by Ethan Hawke. Interestingly, Hawke was inspired to write this book when he discovered that his ancestors were knights with a rich history. Set in the 1300s, the book is centered around the Cornwalls, one of whom left behind writings about mentoring another knight. In it, a young knight, while training with an older knight on the outskirts of town, encounters two different families asking about the town ahead. The first family, loaded up into a wagon with all of their belongings, asks, "What is the town ahead like? We are looking for a place to settle."

In response the older knight asked what they thought of the town they were leaving. Their reply came quickly. "It was terrible. The people were inconsiderate and never helped us when we needed help."

The older knight nodded and said, "To be honest, I think you'll find more of the same ahead of you."

The family frowned and carried on. And as the knight-in-training and his mentor continued to work on the farm, another family came up the road. Their wagon was similarly packed, and they stopped, asking the knights the same question. "We are thinking of moving to the town up ahead. What is it like?"

Again the old knight said, "What did you think of the town you are leaving?"

They answered, "We loved it. It was beautiful and the people were great."

The old knight smiled and said, "To be honest, I think you'll find more of the same ahead of you."

The young knight, confused, asked his mentor why he gave the two families the same answer, even though their past experiences were vastly different. The old night shrugged and said, "Their experience will be affected by their attitude."

We give power to what we focus on. The older knight knew this. Our attitudes and the judgments we make can color our experiences. This is why mindset, more than motivation, affects who we are and what we do. Motivation is a feeling and can be fleeting. A mindset of commitment is steady and unyielding. The sooner we untangle ourselves from the rollercoaster of emotions, the sooner we can focus on growth, success, and happiness. Mindset takes us further than motivation ever can, and it is the cornerstone of our character. This, my friends, is what the great ones know.

CHAPTER 10

TIME TRAVEL IS NOT
YOUR SUPERPOWER

In any given moment, our minds can exist in one of three temporal spaces: the past, the present, or the future.

I know I'm not the first to tell you that living in the past and living in the future is often problematic for our minds. Drifting into the past can generate feelings of frustration, shame, and disappointment, characterized by a lingering sense of "woulda, coulda, shoulda." Or as I like to call it, "Uncle Rico Syndrome"—a reference to the character from Napoleon Dynamite, constantly stuck ruminating on past glories and missed opportunities. Venturing into the future can invoke anxiety, stress, and pressure, permeated by the nagging fear of "what if." We think "What if I can't do this?" or "What if I didn't practice enough?", both of which get in the way of our ability to perform.

In a 1980 Kentucky Derby race, two horses—Great Prospector and Golden Derby—were neck and neck racing to the finish line. Legs pounding, breath heaving, they pushed their abilities to the limits as they neared the end of the race. Great Prospector was ahead, but instead of concentrating on the task at hand, he reached over and bit Golden Derby. Guess who won? It wasn't Great Prospector—he was winning until he bit his opponent. Golden Derby won that race because he didn't lose sight of his goal. We give power to what we focus on. There are always detractors, but when you have a purpose, work your process, and are intentional about your actions, results will follow. Distractions only get in your way.

Traveling to the future and the past are primary distractions we all experience. Our bodies can't follow us in this experience, yet our minds constantly try to travel where our bodies aren't. Control, focus, clarity, and peace comes when our mind is aligned with our body in the present. Staying in the present allows us to actively apply lessons from our past and make choices that positively influence our future.

Much like the jockey guiding his horse, we strive to keep our mental focus on the task at hand, ensuring that our attention doesn't veer off course. Time travel may seem like an attractive superpower, but it's in the here and now where our real power lies.

Time Travel Is an Addiction

You've likely heard high-profile CEOs, star athletes, and top performers say they struggle with stress and anxiety. It seems to come with the territory of success. Almost like it's a checkmark on the road to achieving your dreams. But you don't have to carry stress and anxiety with you to be successful. Stress and anxiety only come knocking when our minds decide to take a detour into what was or what could be.

We've all got our own blooper reels. The meeting where you put your foot in your mouth, or the pivotal game where you missed the shot, or even the awkward moment at that party. But that doesn't mean we should linger on these instances and replay them repeatedly in our minds. And we shouldn't focus on the future either. Mark Twain once said, "I've had a lot of worries in my life, most of which never happened."

Anxiety constricts your blood flow, and allowing it to rule you hampers your ability to perform. You don't have as much blood and oxygen going to the extremities of your body, which means as an athlete you can't move as you need, and as a professional you can't think rationally. Yet, we jump between these two mindsets—future and past—consistently as the events of our world happen around us. It's as though we're always primed to leap into the DeLorean, burn through 1.21 gigawatts, and fly with Doc into the time continuum!

But what if we could harness thoughts of our future and past into an advantage? What if, rather than being a liability, remembering your past or thinking about your future could be transformed into a tool for personal growth and improved performance? The key lies in understanding how we can use our mental travels to inform and influence our present actions rather than allowing them to induce anxiety or regret.

When Time Travel Can Enhance the Current Moment

Your presence in the current moment is preferred, but the past and present can inform the choices you make in that moment. I like to compare it to driving a car in the canyon.

If you were driving down a canyon road, and all you were focused on were the beautiful mountains and the peaks in front of you (the future), you wouldn't make it very far because you would likely run into a wall or drive off a cliff. The same would happen if you were too focused on your rear view mirror (the past), worried about the vehicles behind you and what they were doing.

However, there are times when you should look at what's coming up ahead and check what's happening behind you. But you need to find a safe place (and in our minds, a safe way) to do it. You can dream big for the future and learn from the past, but you can't live in either. You have to live right here, right now. It's where all the magic happens. Be 5% in the past, 5% in the future, and 90% in the moment. That way you can use your past lessons and your future hopes to shape the present moment.

Stay in the Moment

Whenever I got stuck in the past, buried in my mistakes or failures, my mother would always say, "Time to pull out the windshield wiper!" It was her way of telling me to leave these things in the past and move forward. She would make a windshield wiper with her index fingers in front of her eyes and say "Erase, erase, and move forward." It was just silly enough that I would quit thinking about the past so I could move forward.

When I stressed about the future and worried about what I would need to do or what I hadn't yet accomplished, my grandmother would tell me to "Cross that bridge when you get to it." These fears I worried about hadn't happened yet (and might not even happen at all), so I didn't need to consider them until they became a reality.

While the phrases are good to remember, and I hope they help you, they likely have more impact on me than you because I grew up with them.

So here are a few techniques you can use to stay in the moment:

Breathe

So much in this life is about breathing. Studies have shown that breathing techniques reduce anxiety on a significant level if you allow breathing to become part of your daily acumen. Earlier, in chapter five, we talked about "3-2-1 Breathe," but I want to introduce another technique, which was studied by Doctor Hubberman from Stanford.

Remember when you were a kid and started to cry or get angry over what you now understand isn't something worth getting angry about? I'd bet you heard your parents say more than once "Take a deep breath." It does help! So why did we stop doing this as adults? The technique coined by Dr. Hubberman is the "double inhale." It involves a double inhale through the nose followed by a long exhale.

This method can quickly reduce stress levels, and it expels a large amount of carbon dioxide from your system, which means your thoughts are clearer, and you can return to the present moment and perform at a higher level. No matter what you might be doing. There's a direct link between stress levels and performance, and lower stress typically means better performance and increased confidence. As stress and anxiety goes down, performance and confidence goes up, and vice versa.

So when you feel the stress, remember to breathe. Try the double inhale. I myself am on team Hubberman because, let me tell you, this breathwork consistently helps me. I use this breathing technique because it provides instant relief and a sense of rejuvenation in both stressful and relaxed situations. It's like a reset button which recalibrates my focus. I even use this technique in the huddle with my eight-year-old's football team!

Next Best Action (NBA)

In chapter four, we talked about asking yourself "What's important now?" as a powerful way to bring your focus back to the present moment. But another useful question is, "What is my next best action?" or NBA.

The people I work with, who are great at what they do, ask themselves questions like these constantly. They know the power of staying in the present moment, but that doesn't mean they don't get lost in the past and the future (just like the rest of us). The acronym NBA helps them remember to consider their next best action in any given moment. It drives them to consider what they need to do at this moment to get where they want to go.

Asking ourselves "What's important now?" and "What's my next best action?" during a stressful situation means we can focus on tasks we can perform in the present instead of worrying about our past or future. They transform vague worries or thoughts into specific actions so our mind then moves back to the current moment.

Progressive Muscle Relaxation (PMR)

There's an incredible amount of scientific evidence to support that by consciously tightening and relaxing our muscles, we can foster a state of relaxed focus.

So, what is PMR, exactly? It's a process of sequentially tensing and relaxing different muscle groups in your body, starting from your calves and moving all the way up to your face. The idea is to tense a particular muscle group for about twenty seconds and then release, causing a flood of blood to the muscles and inducing a relaxed state.

To put it simply, you start by lying down with your arms and legs uncrossed. Flex your calves as tight as you can, and then tighten them even more. After twenty seconds, you release the tension. With each round, you add on another muscle group. After your calves, it's your quads, then your glutes, your stomach, chest, and finally, your face by pursing your lips and closing your eyes tightly.

After this exercise, shake out your limbs, open your eyes, and you should feel a considerable sense of relaxed focus—a peaceful, centered presence that allows you to concentrate on what truly matters. This technique, while valuable, should not be performed less than 4 hours before a competition as it can make you overly relaxed, possibly lethargic.

An abbreviated version of PMR is called a "body scan," which you can do just five minutes before a competition. You scan your body from head to toe, identifying areas of stress. If your hands are shaky, for instance, you clench your fists and forearms tightly for ten seconds, then release and shake them out, repeating this a few times. This method helps release tension, induce focus, and can be adapted for stress in any part of your body.

The key to mastering these techniques is deep practice and patience. The more you incorporate them into your daily routine, the more you'll adapt them to suit your personal needs. And the better they can help you to stop time traveling away from the present moment.

Meditation

Meditation is one of those things that often gets a bad rap. Many people, myself included, might have dismissed it as some kind of mystical mumbo-jumbo.

I confess, as a former football player and sport psychology student, I was far from being a believer in meditation when my professor discussed it in class. I thought it was some sort of gimmick that came out of the hippie movement in the 1960s. When my sports psychology professor started talking about meditation, I boldly declared, "I think it's bullcrap, and I don't want to use it in my career."

My professor, understanding my skepticism, challenged me to try the app Headspace for forty-two consecutive days (until the end of the semester). If I still didn't believe in it after that, I wouldn't have to incorporate meditation into my practice. I took the challenge, thinking at least I could get it over with and never have to deal with it again.

In the first two weeks, I didn't think much had changed. But then, my wife remarked, "Whatever you're doing right now, I really like this version of Riley." I shrugged it off and continued with the challenge. Another two weeks passed, and friends started to notice a difference in me, saying, "It feels like everything's coming up Riley lately. What are you doing differently?" An odd coincidence, but still, I shrugged it off, sure it had nothing to do with the meditation.

But soon, I began to experience a peace, calm, focus, and clarity I had never felt before. It wasn't something I was used to feeling. It gave me more energy and patience throughout my day, and I was much more present in my life overall. I could no longer shrug off the changes which affected me through meditation. So, I bit the bullet, told my professor she was right, and have been using it ever since.

Give meditation a try. There are plenty of apps like Headspace, Calm, and Breathe that make meditation more accessible and less intimidating. These apps often guide you through the meditation process with soothing voices and easy-to-follow instructions. You don't have to sit in any weird positions or poses. You simply find a quiet place, close your eyes, and listen through the meditation instructions. I've personally found Andy's voice on Headspace to be very relaxing and focusing.

And the best part? These meditation apps cover a range of topics including dealing with adversity, sport performance, overcoming fear, patience, depression, and job loss. My experience turned me from a skeptic to a believer. So, give it a shot—you might just surprise yourself like I did.

Don't Be Afraid of Your Greatness

One final thing to consider: there are times when the very idea of achieving our full potential, our own greatness, can be downright intimidating. It is a part of time traveling into the future that can sometimes hinder progress instead of push it.

Success, in its truest form, isn't just about outdoing others or accumulating accolades and wealth. It's about tapping into the core of who we are and embracing our unique talents. In order to do that, we have to acknowledge our weaknesses and work to improve them. Which is scary! So we end up shrinking ourselves, toning down our brilliance, and playing it safe because we fear what could be.

In those moments, I want you to remember this poem by Marianne Williamson:

Our deepest fear is not that we are inadequate.
Our deepest fear is that we are powerful beyond measure.
It is our light, not our darkness
That most frightens us.
We ask ourselves
Who am I to be brilliant, gorgeous, talented, fabulous?
Actually, who are you not to be?
You are a child of God.
Your playing small
Does not serve the world.
There's nothing enlightened about shrinking
So that other people won't feel insecure around you.
We are all meant to shine,
As children do.
We were born to make manifest
The glory of God that is within us.
It's not just in some of us;
It's in everyone.
And as we let our own light shine,
We unconsciously give other people permission to do the same.
As we're liberated from our own fear,
Our presence automatically liberates others.

Don't let your fear of what could get in the way. Even if the idea of where it could take you is scary. It takes pure unadulterated guts to realize what you could be and strive towards it. The great ones know that fear is expected and don't let themselves shy away from the path because of it.

CHALLENGE 1

For forty-two straight days, try HeadSpace.

CHALLENGE 2

Next time you feel stress or anxiety taking over your thoughts, try the double inhale technique. Breathe in through your nose deeply, then sneak in another deep breath in through your nose, before exhaling in one long breath through your mouth. Now take a moment to study how you feel. Did it help? Where did you feel relief in your body? And if it brought you to the present moment, do you have clarity on your next best action?

CHALLENGE 3

If you find yourself spiraling into the realm of "what ifs" with purely negative thoughts, try to reframe these "what if" with positivity. Instead of "What if I'm not good enough?" Ask yourself, "What if I meet my goals?" or "What if it all works out?" Try and make your "what ifs" more positive with a 5-1 ratio.

CHAPTER 11

ENTHUSIASM OVER ANXIETY

Pat Summitt, an icon in the world of women's basketball, and Tennessee Women's basketball coach once said, "Winning is fun... sure. But winning is not the point. Wanting to win is the point. Never giving up is the point. Never letting up is the point. Never being satisfied with what you've done is the point."[1]

We live in a world that fixates on results and outcomes, and we're often judged by the number of trophies on our shelves or the size of our bank accounts. But what if we changed the narrative? What if winning was less about the end result and more about the journey? What if it was more about the grit, moxie, and perseverance that went into every endeavor?

I love this quote because it changes the scoreboard and redefines what it means to win. No longer is winning about being the first across the finish line, hitting the most home runs, or sinking the final basket. Winning, in its purest form, is the enthusiasm for continuous growth and a steadfast commitment to improvement. It's about the relentless desire to get better and not giving up when the odds are stacked

---

1   (Summitt, 2023)

against us. It's about never settling for what we've accomplished and knowing that there's always another mountain to climb, another goal to chase, another version of ourselves to discover.

This shift in perspective is liberating because no longer is your focus on the win itself. Instead your focus shifts to the process of improvement you take as you develop a skill. When you start to view winning as an ongoing process, rather than a single event, it alleviates the immense pressure that competition often brings. Suddenly, you're no longer solely focused on the prize at the end; you're appreciating the effort, the grind, the sweat, and the tears that go into every challenge. And while winning during this process of improvement is fun, it isn't the point.

One of my most impactful memories came from my 7th grade basketball coach. He taught us the ins and outs of the game and emphasized the importance of improving our skills daily. But the most pivotal lesson I learned came from our team's cheer. Before every game, the coach would have us gather, put our hands in, and shout, "It just doesn't matter!"

As a young boy, I found the cheer cheesy and pointless. The amused chuckles from parents and the grinning faces of my teammates would annoy me. "What's the point of this?" I remember thinking. The cheer seemed demotivating and annoying to me. Why was I trying at all if it didn't matter? But my coach had a very good reason for it, and it wasn't until much later in life that I understood the truth hidden in that seemingly trivial chant. It wasn't the outcome of the game that mattered; it was our collective effort. Despite not being the best team on the court, we faced every match with that cheer on our lips and put our full effort into the game.

And my coach isn't the only one who uses this type of cheer. Shaun White, arguably one of the greatest snowboarders of all time, was asked about his pre-performance routine. In his answer, he discussed a powerful mantra. He said once he gets to the top of the hill, and is about to go down, the last thing he says to himself is, "Who cares. At the end of the day, who cares? What's the big deal? I'm here, I'm going to try my best. And who cares? I'm going to move on from this, regardless of what happens, even though my entire world is wrapped up in this. Who cares?"[2]

White's mantra comes from an understanding of productive self-talk. By uttering these words, he diminishes the gravity of the moment and realigns his focus on the core of his passion: his love for snowboarding. The phrase "Who cares?" acts as a tool which unbinds him from the tension of expectations. It creates emotional distance, allowing for a freer, more genuine performance.

Can you recall a time when you didn't concern yourself with the judgment of others or the potential results? How did that impact your performance? Did you find that your best self emerged when you detached from the outcome? Quite often, when we stop being overly concerned with the outcome, and instead enjoy the thing we love, we liberate our best selves.

When I work with athletes, I often have them use a similar phrase, "So what, now what?" to help them adopt the benefits of this renewed focus. When we can give ourselves just a little bit of space between outcomes and processes, it usually equates to a good outcome. That's the paradox of all of this: letting go of outcomes is a beautiful way to create great outcomes.

---

2   (White, 2023)

In retrospect, I understand why my coach, who by the way is my Dad, chose to have this as our cheer. And now I recognize it as an early introduction to the Achievement Goal Theory. This theory suggests that when an individual is task-oriented, they focus on learning and mastering the task at hand for its own sake. Conversely, when someone is outcome-oriented, their primary objective becomes winning or achieving the end result. The problem arises when people, be they athletes, students, professionals, or even parents, become hyper-focused on outcomes to the extent of losing control over their own actions and emotions.

This is what happens when someone who wants to win so badly, that when they miss a shot or don't catch a ball, they stomp or throw a melt down. They become so over stimulated with anger, and they can't perform. Eckhart Tolle once said, "Don't let a mad world tell you that success is anything other than a successful present moment."[3] The truly great ones—those who exhibit remarkable mental strength and toughness—are task-oriented. So when they miss a shot or don't catch a ball, they focus on their skills in the moment, and not the want of the win itself. They relish in the "lonely work," such as the practice sessions that yield no immediate accolades but pay dividends in the long run. They want to win, but that's not what consumes their mind when they compete. Instead they focus on completing the task to the best of their ability.

---

3   (Tolle, 2021)

Lobster, Crabs, and Frogs—Oh My!

My father had a favorite saying he repeated throughout my childhood, a quote by Winston Churchill: "Never give in, never, never, never." [4]

I never fully understood the wisdom behind these words until my freshman year at Snow College. When I started playing on the football team, I found myself on the bottom, as the fifth-string quarterback. Meaning there were five others ahead of me in the quarterback competition. The beginning was grueling, with my first two passes in our first team scrimmage resulting in interceptions and touchdowns for the defensive squad. Frustrated and disheartened, after only one week of college football, I decided to quit. Football hadn't turned out the way I wanted, and it seemed like I wasn't as good as I thought I was. So, I called my father ready to tell him to come pick me up and take me home. To my surprise, he didn't fight me on it. Instead he said, "Riley, you can quit if you want, and I'll come and get you, but could you give it one more week? If it's still bad by next Saturday, I'll come and pick you up. You just keep bobbin' and weavin' and keep throwing elbows until next week."

His words were hard to hear. I wanted to quit. I cried. But I kept pushing. Long story short, the next week, one of the other quarterbacks quit and went home. I then slipped in front of the fourth string quarterback into the third string quarterback position. The second string quarterback, who was friends with the original third string quarterback (now fourth string), was mad at the decision to make me third string, and it got in his head. By the end of the second week I was a second string quarterback. All my confidence came

---

4   (Churchill, n.d.)

flooding back, and I was reenergized, recalibrated, and refreshed. No one would outwork me, and no one would give more effort than me from that moment on.

When I look at that pivotal moment, I can't believe how different my life would be if I had quit that day. I wouldn't have played college football, or gotten the injury I did, or taken the path that led me to be a mental performance coach, or even write this book! My life might be completely different. But instead of giving up, with a little encouragement to hold on, and because of that moment, I grew.

Often when I speak to my clients, I refer to their pivotal moments as well. I call it your "lobster" moment. Lobsters have a unique way of growing. When their shells become too restrictive, they find a safe spot under a rock, cast off their tight, uncomfortable shell, and produce a new, larger one. This process is extremely stressful and uncomfortable for the lobster, but it's necessary. And as I remember my own "lobster" moment, and see the "lobster" moments of my clients, I am reminded that bravery and courage aren't about being fearless, but instead are about persevering despite your fears. Just like the lobster, we need to embrace the discomfort, because this is where real growth happens. We cannot always control the outcomes in life, but we can control the effort we put in and get comfortable being uncomfortable.

As you grow, there will inevitably be people who try to bring you down. Have you felt this resistance? Where things seem to be looking up for you, or you've begun moving in a better direction, yet someone tries to make you think it isn't good for you? I've experienced this resistance at various points in my life, and it often came from the most unexpected places. For instance, when I began to start varsity as a sophomore in baseball and basketball, many people seemed to be brewing "haterade." The negativity continued when I received a scholarship to Snow College and later signed on to play football at BYU and eventually became the starting quarterback at Utah State University. Whenever this happened, I often found myself complaining to my father about it. Everytime I complained to him about it, he shrugged his shoulders and said, "Crabs in a bucket!"

It was his way of reminding me that there will always be others who try to pull you down. Those who hunt crabs know they can keep them in an open bucket as long as there is more than one crab within that bucket. Every time the other crab tries to escape, one crab will invariably pull the other back in, every time. I saw this happen in real life while walking along a beach in southern France. I observed a man hunting crabs and was mesmerized by the force with which the crabs pulled each other down, preventing each other's escape. There was almost violent opposition in that bucket.

The harder you work, the more successful you become, and the better choices you make, you will feel a similar resistance from other people. Now, not all "crabs" in our lives have malicious intent. Often, they pull us down because they can't envision the grand scope of our dreams or they are uncomfortable with our changes because it means change in their own lives. You might see these in parents, friends, coaches, and even team members.

Not long ago, I had a conversation with a promising college basketball player. He dedicated his summer before senior year to enhancing his physical and mental game, preparing himself for the formidable jump to the NBA. During a break from training in his hometown, his father, who had been diligently rebounding basketballs for him, asked a simple yet weighted question: "What are you going to do after this year?"

The player, a little confused, answered, "I'm going to play in the NBA."

His father, however, responded with another question. "What if that doesn't work out?"

At first glance, this may sound like a typical parental concern for their child's future. Yet, there's more to it. The father's response, although not intended to discourage his son, is meant to pull his son back to the norm of finding a nine to five job instead of pursuing his dream. Sometimes, those who try to keep us in the bucket do so not out of ill-will, but because of their own fears and limitations. They might not know how to dream big or pursue ambitious goals, so they keep us tethered to their reality for their comfort and security.

You can't let that stop you. As Winston Churchill once said, "You will never reach your destination if you stop and throw stones at every dog that barks."[5] So don't let these "crabs" live rent-free in your head. Stay focused on your path and on the daily processes that will lead you to your goals. Remember, resistance is just a sign of your growth, and you have the power to overcome it. When resistance comes, focus on your strengths. The path you are on is a long one, and you need to take it one step at a time.

Mark Twain once said, "Eat a live frog first thing in the morning and nothing worse will happen to you the rest of the day."[6] Chase your dreams, and give yourself one thing you can improve on each morning to get you one step closer.

---

5   (Churchill, n.d.)
6   (Twain, n.d.)

Facing and conquering arduous tasks in the morning can seem daunting, but it's undeniably rewarding. It's a time when you have the most energy and the least distractions. Winning the morning can set you up for a successful day. It's your chance to secure three victories before the workday even begins. Once you enter the workplace, "swallowing the frog" first can pay off. Get the most challenging task out of the way first. You will feel accomplished, and the momentum can carry you through whatever else comes your way, making everything else feel less intimidating.

It's the same way with your dreams. Focus on the hard things first. Take it step by step. If you can complete something each day that inches you closer to your dream, do it. Let your enthusiasm carry you when things get hard. Between shedding your lobster skin, escaping the crabs, and eating the ugly frog, your progress won't be easy or fast. But it will be worth it! Anything worthwhile usually takes a little bit longer and is a little more difficult than originally anticipated.

Don't Discount Enthusiasm

Enthusiasm is a powerful concept with roots that trace back to ancient Greece. The term derives from "en-theos," which literally translates to "gods within" or "divinity within." The ancient Greeks believed that someone filled with enthusiasm was essentially carrying the gods within them.

Think about any significant company, influential person, or esteemed member of society. Isn't there a unique spark of enthusiasm about them? Think about someone you deeply admire. Can you feel the enthusiasm radiating from them? This is something that often unconsciously separates the good from the great. Until we identify enthusiasm, it's not something we know how to put our finger on. But now that you know, think about those in your life who are enthusiastic and those who are not. Which ones would you rather spend more time with?

Working with women, I often encounter feelings of overwhelming pressure to do more, to extend beyond their perceived limits. In such situations, I urge them to understand that they are already enough. They don't need to stretch themselves thin or add more tasks to their already overflowing plate. Rather, they need to shift their perspective and alter their approach. It's not about doing more; it's about doing whatever they are already doing with more enthusiasm. It's a mental adjustment and a different way of participating in the world.

My Grandpa Clark was a paragon of enthusiasm, and though I was merely seven, I could feel his zest for life resonating in every interaction. My mother too exudes a unique enthusiasm. On her birthday, she makes it a point to share candy with everyone she encounters, announcing, "Happy birthday to me!" Her enthusiasm for her special day inadvertently brightens up the day for others as well. The greatest coaches I have worked with display a contagious enthusiasm for their sport. Each one of these individuals possess a unique and inspirational form of enthusiasm.

One fascinating study conducted at Cal Berkeley and Harvard University scrutinized every NBA game played from 2007 to 2011. They specifically examined the impact of "tactile non-verbal enthusiasm."[7] During this period, Steve Nash recorded the highest instances of tactile touch—a powerful non-verbal expression of enthusiasm. Intriguingly, the five championship-winning teams in those years had the highest

7   (Kraus, Huang, & Keltner, 2010)

frequency of such touches. Even in the face of seemingly impossible odds, the Dallas Mavericks overcame Lebron James and his squad in 2011, registering a four to one advantage in tactile touching.

Enthusiasm extends far beyond verbal expressions. It can be conveyed in countless non-verbal, complimentary ways. Science has even highlighted the benefits of enthusiasm in overcoming disappointing performances.

Studies show that becoming focused on others and radiating enthusiasm towards them is the most effective way to shrug off a poor performance and uplift your spirits. It enables you to metaphorically put a period at the end of a disappointing sentence, allowing you to move on to the next with renewed enthusiasm. This can be a high five or an encouraging word. But whatever you do, it shifts you away from focusing on the negative and encourages positive thinking. Because when you have a bad session, competition, or game, if you can turn toward others, you can become extrinsically focused instead of intrinsically focused.

I recall a particularly inspiring instance of enthusiasm in action during my time with Philip Rivers, the famed NFL quarterback, during the 2002 season at North Carolina State. Years after coaching at North Carolina State University, I found myself watching Rivers play against the Kansas City Chiefs in his fifteenth NFL season. In that game, he led the Chargers to a stunning victory over the highly skilled Chiefs and their formidable quarterback Patrick Mahomes. Throughout the game, I was persistently rooting for Rivers. His love for the game, his team, and his coaching staff was infectious. He was a pivotal player for everyone who worked with him.

Rivers's enthusiasm wasn't limited to his performance on the field. In a post-game interview, he expressed belief in his teammates, coaches, system, himself, and his offensive line. He praised Mahomes, the opposing team's quarterback, as well as the Kansas City team and their coaches. Despite making mistakes during the game, including two early interceptions, Rivers remained undeterred, embodying the enthusiasm that characterizes a championship-level quarterback.

There are two key takeaways here: First, never underestimate the power of a well-timed, genuine and authentic compliment. Rivers's compliments extended beyond his team to include his opponents which was a testament to his character. Secondly, perfection isn't the goal; it's about maintaining the will to battle, swing hard, and keep playing, despite any missteps along the way.

Since 2002, I have thought about Phillip Rivers a lot. I constantly analyze why he was a champion and why I liked him so much. The reason why Phillip is such a pleasure to watch, and the reason I love being around him, comes down to enthusiasm. He plays as if he's aflame, his zeal influencing not just his teammates and coaches, but his family. His unique, contagious enthusiasm is something rare, a characteristic that sets him apart, and to harness that level of enthusiasm is a noble pursuit, not only in sports but in every aspect of life.

Turn Down the Volume

In our pursuit of success, we frequently encounter a common adversary: anxiety. Most of our anxiety comes when our mind is turned up to max volume. For many of us, when we compete, the volume is a 10 (on a scale from 1 to 10), which is unhelpful.

But anxiety doesn't have to be viewed as unhelpful. In fact, a little bit of anxiety is *good* for peak-level performance. But it has to be just the right amount. Like the three bears, it can't be too much, and it can't be too little, it has to be just right. I want you to think about a couple of high stress situations. First, think about a time where you performed well in a high stress situation. Between 1 and 10, where was your anxiety volume? Second, think about a time which required you to perform well, but you didn't. Now where was your anxiety volume? These two instances likely had very different levels of anxiety.

For myself, I perform best at a four. Some athletes I work with perform better at a two, and others perform better at an eight. But that doesn't mean you will walk into "go" time at your best number. The great ones know how to turn the volume down or to turn the volume up when needed because they understand their optimal number for performance.

If you come into competition at an eight, and you know your number is a five, my advice would be to focus on your breathing, using it to turn the volume down. But if you walk into a competition at a five, and you know you perform best at an eight, I'd recommend listening to a pump up playlist. You can control this number to help you perform better. Another great strategy is to use comedy within your pre-performance routine. Many CEOs of major companies use this before going on stage, and major athletic competitors use it to get loose before a big game. They will listen to a comedy routine before doing something big because it puts a smile on their face and makes them relaxed but not too relaxed.

Sometimes we make the mistake of thinking that stress or pressure are not good for us. But in truth, they are good for us, to a point. When it gets too loud, you need to turn down the volume to perform better. Take a look at this chart. It shows that optimal performance is often between a state of relaxation and a state of anxiety.

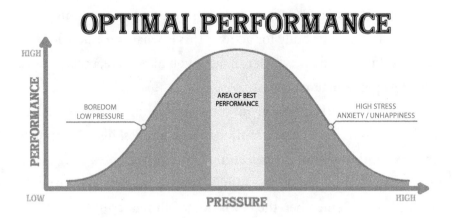

This balance is where we find the Goldilocks zone I mentioned above. Not too much, not too little, but just the right amount of each. We in sports psychology call this the optimal performance zone.

If you're too relaxed, you might lack the necessary motivation, energy, and focus to perform at your best. You might find yourself lethargic, indifferent, or even disinterested, none of which are conducive to peak performance. On the other hand, too much anxiety can be equally detrimental. It can lead to excessive tension, nervousness, and overthinking that can significantly impair your performance. Your thoughts might become clouded and your decision-making flawed, and your actions might not reflect your true potential.

However, a certain degree of both relaxation and anxiety is essential for peak performance. A level of relaxation helps maintain composure, manage stress, and conserve energy. It allows you to stay grounded and focused, enabling a clearer perspective of the task at hand.

On the other hand, a degree of anxiety, often seen as a response to a perceived challenge or threat, can be beneficial. It sharpens your senses, heightens your awareness, and pumps adrenaline into your system, priming your body for action. This is what some people refer to as "productive" stress, which can drive you to prepare, practice, and ultimately perform at your best.

To consistently perform in your optimal zone, it's crucial to develop self-awareness and emotional regulation skills. Techniques such as mindfulness, visualization, controlled breathing, and progressive muscle relaxation can help manage anxiety and promote a relaxed state. Remember, the key is not to eliminate anxiety entirely but to keep it within manageable limits while fostering a relaxed yet focused mindset. This balance is part of the art and science of performance. It's about knowing yourself, recognizing your emotional and physiological responses, and skillfully adjusting your mindset and state to perform at your peak, regardless of the situation.

This is a pivotal lesson I learned at a very young age. On the way to a little league football state championship, I shared with my mother how nervous I was. She simply smiled and said, "Good. I'd be worried about you if you weren't nervous."

Anxiety isn't your enemy. It's perfectly okay to feel anxious. It means you care about what you're doing. The trick is not to let anxiety control you. Instead, acknowledge it, normalize it, and harness its energy to fuel your performance. Try naming and thanking it for showing up. Tell anxiety to get some popcorn ready while you perform. Then invite your anxiety to sit back and watch as you rise to the occasion. This way, you're transforming it from an overpowering force into a spectator in your performance. You have the power to turn your anxiety into enthusiasm. And by adjusting the volume, you'll find the right amount of anxiety that makes you shine!

CHALLENGE 1

Add an extra level of enthusiasm to your regimen. Add an intention of enthusiasm to everything you do today. If you are working out, put a little more enthusiasm into it. If you are working, put a little more enthusiasm into it. If you are playing, put a little more enthusiasm into it.

CHALLENGE 2

The next time you're facing a stressful situation or event, ask yourself, "Who cares?" This mindset might just be the key to turning down the volume on your anxiety and unlocking your highest potential.

CHALLENGE 3

Try to identify your peak performance level number, 10 being so stressed you are shaking, and 1 being you could fall asleep. Where on the scale do you perform best? Now that you've identified this number, try strategies such as music, comedy, and breathing to adjust this number as needed.

CHAPTER 12

KEY TEAM DYNAMICS

Team dynamics significantly impact the performance and success of a group, whether it's on a sports field, in an office, or any other setting where teamwork is crucial. Forming a team who trusts and relies on each other is not easy, and when things get tough, many walk away and figure if the team isn't "working," then the team itself probably shouldn't be together.

However, when you understand key team dynamics, you aren't relying on the "newness" or motivation to keep the team together. Instead, you understand that working as a collective does not happen easily or slowly, but rather in four distinct stages which you can recognize as your team matures and strives to find that final smooth sailing transition into effective and efficient teamwork.

The team itself must go through four stages: Forming, Storming, Norming, and Performing.

Forming

The Forming stage occurs when a team initially comes together. During this phase, team members try to understand each other, build relationships, and identify commonalities. The team is essentially laying the groundwork for collaboration and developing an ethos of playing for one another. During this forming stage, trust and commonalities are built through the sharing of stories. We are more likely to be a better team if we can find commonalities within our stories, and most of us are more alike than we think. We can almost always find a story that would help us play for the person next to us.

If you're a sports movie enthusiast, you've probably seen the film "Hoosiers" about the Hickory High School Huskers from a remote town in Indiana. In my mind, it perfectly embodies the initial stage of team development. In this movie, individuals with varying skills and backgrounds come together, not yet as a team, but as a motley crew of aspiring champions. In the beginning, it's a delicate dance of introductions, initial assessments, and anxious uncertainty. But during these assessments, the foundational values, norms, and roles which will guide the team's future trajectory are formed.

Forming is not about instant harmony; it's about creating an environment for mutual understanding. In the movie, Coach Dale understood this. He employed a variety of strategies, from tough love to inspirational speeches, gradually earning the respect and trust of his players and the community. And it is here we find the secret sauce of forming—patience. Coach Dale provided a space for individuals to express their fears, doubts, and aspirations, all while setting expectations and defining roles. He created a shared vision for the team.

Forming is not a linear path. It is full of progress and setbacks, small victories and minor defeats. Coach Dale's story was no different. His efforts to change the team's playing style were met with resistance. His stern demeanor led to clashes. His past raised doubts. Yet, through this tumultuous journey, the team began to come together, marking the end of forming and the onset of storming.

A well-managed forming stage can create a robust foundation for team performance. It nurtures trust, encourages communication, and promotes cohesion—all vital elements for achieving collective success. The Hickory Huskers, once disorganized, evolved into a high-performing team that went on to win the state championship. When you enter into any new team, pay attention to the forming stage, nurture it, be patient with it, and most importantly, value it.

Storming

Following Forming comes the Storming stage, a phase of competition and conflict as team members start vying for positions and roles within the team. This can sometimes result in friction or misunderstandings, but it's an integral part of the process as it enables individuals to define their contributions and assert their capabilities.

In 2001, Allen Iverson, the diminutive giant of the NBA, experienced a rough patch with his teammates. Coach Larry Brown, the tough-as-nails strategist of the 76ers, had a tough task at hand. Iverson was not just another player; he was the fulcrum, the alpha and the omega of the team. The team couldn't succeed without him, yet they couldn't seemingly exist with him. They were experiencing the rough highs and lows of "storming."

Think of storming like a chef trying to create a new recipe. The ingredients don't always agree with each other, leading to a culinary conflict. Each element has its unique flavor, which it wants to express, but the chef's ultimate goal is to achieve a harmonious blend. Team dynamics in sport, as in the kitchen, can be just as volatile and delicately balanced.

With Iverson and the 76ers, their storming phase was magnified by the relentless scrutiny of the media and fans. Iverson's unconventional playing style clashed with Brown's structured approach, leading to a series of confrontations, missed practices, and on-court tensions. But beneath this apparent chaos, something was evolving. Both were uncompromising characters, yet they needed to work together, so they stepped into a meeting together. In that meeting, they aired out their grievances, their hopes, and most importantly, their mutual goal of winning the championship.

Progression from storming to norming happens when teams find common ground amidst their differences. It's about recognizing that individual talents are subservient to team success. When Iverson and Brown emerged from that meeting, the 76ers were not just a group of talented individuals anymore; they had started to morph into a collective unit, with each part working for the whole.

The rest of the season saw a rejuvenated Iverson, a calmer Brown, and a more unified 76ers. They stormed through the rest of the NBA, ending the season with Iverson winning the MVP and the 76ers reaching the NBA Finals. Storming, while often uncomfortable, is vital for any team, regardless of the nature of the sport or the scope of the goal. It's a challenging phase, but only through the storm can teams find their true compass.

Norming

Norming involves the acceptance of individual roles, establishment of team norms, and the alignment of team members towards a common goal. During this stage, everyone begins to understand and appreciate their unique contributions and the value they bring to the team.

Back in 1980, during the Cold War, tensions were high at the Winter Olympics in New York. The underdog American hockey team was about to face the seemingly invincible Soviet Union squad. But, the American hockey team of collegiate players would make history, showcasing the power of "norming." This team was an amalgamation of players from rival colleges. Their initial sessions were marred by regional animosities, individual ego clashes, and lack of trust—a storming phase in its full glory. However, by the time the Olympics came their way, they had transformed into a cohesive "norming" team.

A well-normed team functions like a well-oiled machine, where each part knows its role and trusts others to do theirs, creating an ensemble of seamless cooperation. The impact of norming on the performance of the 1980 U.S. Olympic Hockey Team was evident in the "Miracle on Ice," where this united squad defeated the Soviet team. Their victory was a testament to their unity, their shared consciousness, their unwavering commitment to their collective goal.

The strength of a team is not just in the skills of its individuals, but in the harmony of their collective. At the end of the day, it's the teams that master the art of norming who create miracles. These teams carry one another, pick each other up when they are down, and act as an individual source of motivation and inspiration beyond our own selfish interests.

Performing

This stage is the sweet spot where team synergy is at its peak. As each individual embraces their role, the team's collective output often surpasses the sum of its parts. This is the stage where the team's full potential is realized and high performance is achieved. But, and this is a big but, they cannot do so unless they move through all four of these stages. Just like the shire horse who can pull more the longer they work together, the combined strength of the team can far exceed individual capabilities when the team has moved through all four stages collectively.

The U.S. Men's Basketball Team, more popularly known as the "Dream Team," is a group of NBA stars who were a constellation of extraordinary talents. This team, composed of NBA greats such as Michael Jordan, Larry Bird, Magic Johnson, and others, was more than just a collection of outstanding individual players. They were the epitome of performance. And yet, almost no one saw them play together. When they did, it wasn't in a game for a championship or a medal, but an intra-squad scrimmage referred to as "The Greatest Game Nobody Ever Saw." In this practice match, the Dream Team was divided into two, with Magic Johnson leading one side and Michael Jordan the other. The game was an intense showcase of individual talent, strategy, and competitiveness, but what stood out was the seamless chemistry, the unspoken understanding, and the collective commitment towards shared growth. It was a display of performing in its purest form.

The Dream Team, in their journey through the Olympics, showcased this amplified performance. They dominated the tournament, winning by an average margin of forty-four points, and clinched the gold medal.

The performing phase is the culmination of all prior stages. It's the stage where team members have forged their identities within the group, negotiated their differences, and accepted their roles. They have become more than just a team; they are a cohesive unit with a shared consciousness, a collective that is in tune with each other's strengths and weaknesses. A team in the performing stage is like an orchestra where every instrument plays in perfect harmony, enhancing the overall melody.

As an individual, understanding these stages is vital because it allows you to predict and manage your reactions throughout the team's evolution. For instance, during the Storming stage, you might face competition and confrontations. This is a natural part of the process, and recognizing that can help you remain composed and focused on your performance, rather than taking things personally. In the Norming stage, understanding that your role is now defined, regardless of your initial expectations, is crucial. It's about being the best player for your team, even if you are not the best player on your team. Everyone can contribute uniquely to a team's success, and sometimes, being the best player on the team without being the best player for the team can actually be detrimental to the group's overall harmony and productivity.

When you find yourself in your own head and feeling demotivated because you didn't like something you did or how something was handled on your team, remember the goal of the overall collective. You'll be surprised at how often remembering the collective goal is a motivator in and of itself which forces you to consider how best you can serve the team.

Trust Versus Performance

While performance can secure a short-term win, it's the balance of trust and performance that ensures long-term success. It allows teams to weather storms and evolve together, fostering an environment where everyone can be the best player for the team. Simon Sinek emphasizes the value of trust within a team, comparing it to the importance of trust in the military. In such high-stakes situations, trust goes beyond merely trusting someone with your life; it extends to trusting them with your most valuable possessions and personal relationships.

The comparison Sinek draws between "high performance" and "high trust" is particularly unique. He suggests that high performance alone, without the foundation of trust, can be detrimental to team dynamics.

Consider the individual in your office who is highly skilled but unreliable or untrustworthy. This person may produce excellent work but at the cost of team harmony and collaboration. In the long run, this creates a toxic environment that impedes team growth and success. In contrast, a team member who may not be the highest performer but is consistently reliable and trustworthy can significantly contribute to the team's cohesion and collective progress. This is a prime example of being the best player for your team instead of being the best player on your team. An optimal team has a blend of high performance and high trust, ensuring sustainable success and team growth.

CHALLENGE 1

What is the overall goal of your current team? Whether work, players, or another team, write down this goal and put it somewhere you can see. When you are feeling a lack of motivation or frustration, review this goal and ask yourself, how can you be the best player for your team?

CHAPTER 13

POWER OF THE REFRAME

Don't think of a pink elephant.

Impossible right?

That's because our minds naturally want to create a mental image for the concept we are given. Regardless of the "don't" preceding the phrase, the image of a pink elephant came to your mind right away. It's only after the image of a pink elephant comes to mind that we remember we shouldn't be thinking of a pink elephant. So instead we think of a pink flamingo or a gray elephant, anything to stop us from thinking of that pink elephant.

This is reframing.

When trying not to think of a pink elephant, you reframe your thinking into something else as soon as your brain remembers that a pink elephant shouldn't be on your mind. This might be easy to do with an elephant, but what about when you are filled with doubt, frustration, or even fear? Just like the pink elephant, we know we shouldn't let these things block our thought process, but reframing isn't as easy in those situations.

A few years ago, I had the privilege to work with a powerful baseball player. When he connected with the ball, it would often result in a double, triple, or even a home run. But he was striking out too much. He told me he would do anything to hit the ball more often. As we looked at his situation, I asked him to walk me through his process when he approached the plate. He said, "Well, I look at the label on my bat, take a deep breath, and imagine myself hitting the baseball. Then, right as I step into the box to hit the ball, I say to myself: don't strike out."

Talk about a pink elephant! By saying those words, he was imagining himself striking out just as clearly as you imagined a pink elephant. Even if he didn't want that image in his mind, and he didn't want that result, thinking of the possibility of that outcome was interfering with his performance.

Together, we reframed this mantra. I asked him, "Can we solve the problem of not striking out without using the words 'strike out'?" He thought about it, and told me he wished he could repeatedly make "solid contact" with the ball. Perfect! Now every time he walks up to the plate, he uses the power phrase "solid contact" instead of "don't strike out." These two phrases paint a vastly different picture, don't they? After he changed this phrase, he hit the ball consistently and powerfully.

This can work in every area of your life. Right before a presentation, instead of saying, "Don't screw it up," say to yourself, "Go give a great presentation." When I work with quarterbacks, instead of saying, "Don't throw an interception in the red zone," I say, "Take care of the football." That subtle change makes a big difference. It helps you visualize the positive action you want to take, rather than the negative action you're trying to avoid. In essence, we start to play to win, rather than playing to not lose.

The phrases we say to ourselves play a monumental role in how our minds visualize actions and outcomes. A positive reminder or power phrase allows us to shift our mindset and focus on the results we want, not the ones we fear.

Reframing Your Life

Not all of our thoughts are true. They're merely perspectives, and perspectives can be reframed. Every day, I make an effort to choose happiness, gratitude, and contentment and frame my life in a manner that uplifts both myself and others.

This isn't something that comes easy. In my forties, I could have thought of my life in one of two ways:

Scenario 1: I'm a forty-year-old father of two young children, with three different jobs in the past year alone. I've had my fair share of failures and disappointments, like being benched during my senior year as the starting QB at Utah State University. I've worked seven different jobs in sixteen years, and have been overlooked for leadership positions because I was single for a long time. I bought my first house at thirty, seemingly lagging behind my peers, many of whom had advantages I didn't seem to have. At present, I find myself unemployed and caring for the kids while my wife works to keep us afloat.

Scenario 2: I'm incredibly fortunate. I'm a loving husband and a proud father, with a supportive and accomplished wife. I was able to fulfill my dream of playing quarterback in college, graduating with honors, and later even coaching at the college level. I've been surrounded by inspirational people and have had unique opportunities, like coaching Phillip Rivers. I currently co-own a company, Mountain West Elite, and have the freedom to work from home while pursuing a degree in Sport and Performance Psychology. I see nothing but bright skies ahead.

Which scenario was true at forty? Both. Each paints an accurate picture of my life at that time. But which perspective is more beneficial? Without a doubt, scenario two. We empower the narratives we choose to focus on, and I chose to see my life through a more optimistic and grateful lens. That's not to say that scenario one is false, but it isn't helpful.

The question now is, how do you frame your life? Are you a source of positivity or negativity? You can depict your life as a horror film or a love story. When you consistently choose to recognize joy, you will enjoy your life more. No matter the situation, the power of reframing is always within your grasp. Your life's narrative is yours to write. Choose wisely. Choose positivity.

Self-Imposed Prisons

Have you ever been to a circus?

Picture dazzling lights illuminating colorful tents. The lingering aroma of popcorn and cotton candy wafting through the air. The sound of laughter and chatter echoing around you. And you have just been invited to peek into the back, inner workings of a circus show before the performance starts.

Inside the back of the tent, the performers are busily preparing their costumes, and various exotic animals, from chattering monkeys to lions pacing in their cages, contribute to the chaos. But amid the flurry of activity, one sight grabs your attention: an immense elephant. Though he is larger and likely stronger than anything in the tent, he is held in place by nothing more than a meager rope tied loosely around his ankle.

Naturally, you might ask a nearby circus worker why the elephant doesn't break free. The worker, barely looking up from his work, would respond, "He could. But he won't."

You see, this elephant, who could effortlessly uproot trees or trample fences, has been conditioned to believe that the rope can restrain him. As a young calf, the elephant had tried and failed to break the rope, and over time, had grown to accept that escape was impossible. Even though as he grew he gained the strength to break it, the mental barrier and belief that he could not hold him back from freedom.

In many ways, just like this elephant, we tend to limit our own possibilities. Especially when we accept our thoughts and perceived restraints as truth. These self-limiting beliefs can manifest as thoughts like, "I'm not talented enough," or "I can't handle the pressure," or "I will never achieve my dreams." Just like the elephant, by continually reinforcing these beliefs, we convince ourselves they are immovable truths, when in reality, they are nothing more than figments of our own imagination.

Do not let yourself be captured within a self-imposed prison. Like the elephant, we are far more powerful than the frail ropes we believe bind us. But to break free of them, we first have to recognize and accept these mental barriers.

Reframe Your Messaging

By recognizing and discarding the limiting language of absolute words, we empower ourselves to reshape our mindset, our behavior, and our reality. Here are four steps you can take to reframe your language:

1. **Awareness**: Recognize when you're falling into the trap of using these definitive words. These phrases usually surface when you're reacting to a particular stressful situation. Remember: there's a gap between your feelings and the words you choose to express them.

2. **Questioning**: Confront these definitive statements with three questions: Where did this thought originate from? Is it true? Is it helping me? If the answer to any of these questions is troubling, discard the statement immediately.

3. **Look for Exceptions**: For example, if you often say, "Every time I get nervous, I mess up," reflect on the accuracy of that statement. Upon closer examination, you'll find numerous instances when you were nervous yet still performed well.

4. **Reframe**: Work to combat unproductive self-talk by reframing the words you use. Just as the baseball player changed "don't strike out" to "make solid contact with the ball," you need to consciously replace and reframe definitive words like this:

Always—Sometimes

Never—Rarely

Every time—Frequently

Everybody—Many people

Nobody—Some people

All—Many

By softening these absolute terms, you open up new possibilities that were previously unseen. You become naturally more optimistic because you see opportunities you hadn't seen before.

This isn't just about self-improvement; it's about the energy you bring to your environment. When you model optimistic, possibility-driven language, others catch on. Not only will these steps help you personally, but these new phrases and attitudes are contagious. Imagine the possibilities if we avoided these types of words on a daily basis?

Here are a few more examples of this powerful tool in action:

Negative thought: "I'm not fast enough."

Reframed: "I'm getting faster. With the progress I've made in the last year, I'm well on track to reach my speed goals."

Negative thought: "I throw too many interceptions in the clutch."

Reframed: "I'm a fast learner. Every level of football has presented its challenges, and I've triumphed at each one. I am getting better every day."

Negative thought: "I don't look like a volleyball player."

Reframed: "Volleyball players come in all shapes and sizes. The best in the sport have diverse body types, and my physical appearance doesn't determine my ability to excel."

Negative thought: "I don't belong in this stadium."

Reframed: "Of course I belong! Every match, every practice is an opportunity to grow and learn. Today could be my breakthrough day."

Your daily thoughts have the potential to either sap your energy or boost it. This is why choosing your words, both in internal self-talk and external conversation, is crucial. By reframing your thoughts, you're taking an active role in your mental well-being and performance. You're transforming potentially damaging narratives into affirmations of continuous growth. And you are choosing daily to cultivate thoughts that have a positive impact on your life.

Lengthen Your Timeline

It's easy to get caught up in the rat race. As young people, we're often driven by a sense of urgency to succeed. We're eager to score the winning goal, to ace the test, to go viral on social media, or to land that dream job. But what if this rush is actually slowing us down rather than propelling us forward? A different approach, one that seems counterintuitive but is backed by some of the greatest success stories, suggests that we might achieve more by taking our foot off the accelerator.

What if, instead of rushing to the finish line, we took the time to appreciate the journey? What if we chose to play the long game, settling in for a marathon rather than a sprint?

It's tempting to seek instant gratification and to yearn for immediate success. We live in a world where viral stars are born overnight and young entrepreneurs make headlines. But remember, for every overnight success, there are countless others who found their breakthrough after years of persistence and perseverance. They took the time to learn, grow, and develop their skills. They committed to their craft and honed it until they excelled.

Before becoming the iconic Han Solo or Indiana Jones, Harrison Ford was a carpenter. In 1964, Ford arrived in Hollywood with the same ambition shared by many others—to become an actor. Amidst a sea of young actors, Ford noticed most were in a hurry to make it, driven by the desire for fame, money, or validation. So, Ford chose a different path. He lengthened his timeline.

Ford became a carpenter, providing an alternative income that allowed him to wait it out in Hollywood. As the years rolled by, many of his peers dropped off the radar, thinning the competition. Being a carpenter also offered Ford unforeseen advantages—he became known as the "carpenter to the stars," which allowed him to build relationships with influential people in Hollywood. This eventually led to Ford being asked to read with other actors for a small film—Star Wars. And his ability to stick it out led to the role of Han Solo.

Ford's strategy can be seen as a civilian version of "winning through attrition," a military tactic of outlasting the enemy rather than defeating them directly. Historian B.H. Liddell Hart found that a mere 2% of historical battles were won as a result of a direct attack, and that many instead were won through attrition. Meaning that Ford's story is not an isolated one. Many others have found the consistency that comes with continued effort often leads to success. Take for example the renowned designer Vera Wang, who didn't design her first dress until she was forty. Before she became the queen of talk shows, Oprah Winfrey was fired from her job at twenty-three—a required stepping stone on her journey to success.

Lengthening our timeline changes our perspective on the journey. It makes us focus less on immediate success and more on long-term growth. Moreover, adopting a "long game" perspective helps us persist even when things get tough. And the idea of "I better pack a lunch because I'll be here all day" embodies this mentality—it implies settling in, being patient, and being ready for the long haul rather than the quick battle. And as we've seen with Ford, Wang, and Winfrey, this approach not only leads to personal growth but often leads to extraordinary outcomes as well.

Paradigm Shifts

Have you heard of Scottie Scheffler? He recently won the Masters Golf Tournament, but it wasn't easy for him. Standing at the brink of his first major victory, the morning of his final day, Scheffler was overwhelmed with stress and confessed to his wife Meredith, "I don't think I'm ready for this. I'm not ready, I don't feel like I'm ready for this kind of stuff."

But his wife asked, "Who are you to say that you are not ready?" And she went on to add "Today won't change how much I love you, how much our kids love you, how we feel about you."

With her help, Scheffler moved from a mindset of fear and self-doubt to one of potential and self-belief. He started to see himself not just as a contender but as a champion, worthy of competing for and winning one of the most prestigious prizes in golf. Taking her words to heart, Scheffler wrote himself a note to help maintain his composure and steadiness on the course, and before every tournament, he would read it.

Here is what it said: "If I win this gold tournament, it will change my life on the golf course. But it won't change my personal life at home. Winning the golf tournament isn't going to satisfy my soul or my heart. I know that going in, so I am able to play freely, knowing that the rest isn't really up to me. I'm just going to do my best."

His new mindset provided him the resilience and mental toughness required to handle the challenges on the course and become a Masters champion! Which wouldn't have been possible without a major paradigm shift.

Our journeys are seldom smooth. We face fears, self-doubt, insecurities, frustration, and much more along the path to success. But champions aren't born—they're made. They're often made from the reforging of their trials and tribulations into stepping stones for success. That's the power of reframing—turning each setback into a comeback, transforming each failure into a lesson, and seeing every challenge as an opportunity.

So, if you find yourself standing at the precipice, staring at a challenge that threatens to unravel your confidence, remember, you have the power to change the narrative. Mia Hamm, one of the most influential women's soccer players in history, faced numerous hurdles on her path to greatness. Rather than succumbing to the limitations of her circumstances, Hamm chose to reframe adversity as an opportunity for personal and athletic development.

With each challenge she encountered, Hamm rewrote the narrative in her mind, transforming setbacks into stepping stones towards mastery. She viewed defeats as valuable lessons, nurturing her relentless pursuit of improvement. Through this reframing process, Hamm unlocked her true potential and propelled herself to Olympic gold medals and World Cup victories, inspiring a generation of aspiring athletes in the process.

The next time you find yourself thinking, "I can't do this," try asking yourself, "How can I do this?" Reframe the question, and you may be surprised at the answer you'll find.

Embracing a paradigm shift isn't just about changing your thoughts; it's about changing your world. It's about embracing the paradigm shift and understanding that your greatest challenges can be your greatest assets. Who knows, the next time you face adversity, instead of seeing an impassable mountain, you may just see your next big climb.

Understanding the potential of reframing is one thing, but harnessing its power is another. Here are some key steps:

1. **Perception Awareness**: Recognize negative thoughts, emotions, and limiting beliefs that hinder your performance. This heightened self-awareness serves as the foundation for reframing.
2. **Cognitive Flexibility**: Embrace the idea that obstacles are opportunities in disguise. Train your mind to explore alternative perspectives and challenge conventional notions of success and failure.
3. **Narrative Reconstruction**: Reconstruct the stories you tell yourself about challenges and setbacks. Instead of seeing them as roadblocks, view them as springboards for growth, resilience, and personal development.
4. **Mental Resilience**: Cultivate an unwavering belief in your ability to reframe and overcome adversity. Build mental toughness by continuously adapting your mindset to changing circumstances.

In the end, we aren't defined by the challenges we face, but by how we choose to perceive and respond to them.

CHALLENGE 1

What is a negative thought which constantly pops up in your mind? It could be about work, or personal challenges, athletic performance, or something else. Whatever it may be, find a way to reframe that thought positively. And practice using it until it becomes your new mantra.

CHAPTER 14

CULTIVATE GROWTH MINDSET

Have you heard the word "Kaizen"?

Kaizen originates from Japan and emerged in the post-World War II era. It combines the Japanese words "kai" (change) and "zen" (good), meaning "change for the better" or "continuous improvement."

In the 1950s, Kaizen took shape as a management philosophy in Japan. The renowned Japanese management consultant, Masaaki Imai, played a significant role in popularizing and spreading the concept globally. In 1986, Imai published the book "Kaizen: The Key to Japan's Competitive Success," which detailed Kaizen principles and practices. The core of which included continuous improvement, continuous learning, and a high focus on quality.

It's an easy reminder of the importance of perpetually learning. After my college graduation, before I went back to school to be in sport psychology, I experienced some fixed mindset in many aspects of my life. It led to stagnation in some of my life goals and in the things I tried to do. I wasn't as open to learning as I had been in the past, and I didn't feel I needed to make much change in my life. However, as I slowly began to realize my dreams were elsewhere and I needed to go back to college, I shifted into a growth mindset. Even now, I'm considering a doctorate, partially because it can give me more success and open doors, but mostly because it would lead to continuous growth in my field.

Growth Versus Fixed Mindset

If you think of mindset as a spectrum, there are typically two distinct sides. The first is known as a "fixed mindset"—it hinges on the belief that one's abilities are unchangeable entities akin to eye color. Conversely there exists a "growth mindset" characterized by understanding that abilities function similarly to muscles—they can be developed and strengthened with persistent effort over time.

Those who possess a growth mindset exude extraordinary levels of grit and moxie. Unaffected by challenges put before them, they view challenges as opportunities for personal education and advancement. They are not the type to give up easily and they maintain an unwavering belief in their capacity to achieve goals as they perceive their abilities as fluid and malleable rather than fixed or rigid.

Dr. Carol Dweck, the author of "Mindset," discusses the impact of mindset on our lives. And one of her compelling arguments revolves around how we praise and encourage our children.

For example, when a child aces their math test, our typical reaction might be to exclaim, "You're so smart!" While this seems like a confidence-boosting compliment, it can actually foster a fixed mindset. When you praise the child's inherent talent or intelligence, you're suggesting that their success is a result of innate ability, instead of hard work. And when they encounter people who seem "smarter," they may feel threatened, doubting their own capabilities and even questioning their worth.

But, if you shift the focus from talent to effort, and instead say something like, "Wow, you must have worked really hard to get that score," you nurture a growth mindset. With those words, you highlight the power of persistence, hard work, and the process of learning itself. You send a message that success is not solely a result of inborn talent but of dedication and effort. When you use this language, you encourage kids (and adults alike) to stick with their endeavors, knowing that they can improve and grow, just like they have in the past. They're not defined by their current abilities but by their potential to become even better.

Nobody is born with a fixed or growth mindset; both are learned. These two mindsets are also not mutually exclusive. You could have a fixed mindset in one area of your life and a growth mindset in another. So, if you find yourself leaning towards a fixed mindset, don't worry. Like any muscle, the growth mindset can be developed with regular exercise and a hearty dose of resilience. With my own children, I focus on hard work and effort. I compliment courage and bravery instead of talent. Because there will be a day in their life when everyone else is just as talented as them, and when that happens, I don't want them to take their ball and go home.

I remember a specific example of this with my daughter, Alexis. With her growing interest in basketball, I decided to take Alexis to tryouts for a team named "Premier." I knew this team would push her limits. The goal wasn't necessarily for her to make the team, but to give her a sense of where she stood amongst her peers. However, the tryouts were far more intense than I'd anticipated. Alexis faced tough competition—the ball was continually stolen from her and her shots almost always blocked. She was struggling. The other girls were highly talented. The longer it went on, the more painful it was for me to watch my daughter fail so hard.

When the tryouts ended, I pulled her close, expressed my love for her, and tried to cushion the inevitable disappointment. I quietly tossed the tryout and team information into the garbage because I knew she wouldn't make the team. When we got to the car, her lip was quivering and she said, "Is it okay if I play junior Jazz the rest of my life?" I wanted to cry with her because I knew exactly how she felt, but instead I said, "Yes, it is okay if you play junior Jazz the rest of your life, but today is not the day to make that decision."

We made it through that hard day, and the next week I continually received a phone call from a number my phone didn't recognize. So, I ignored the call, opting instead to spend time with my kids. After several calls from the same number, I eventually picked up. It turned out to be the coach from Premier. I was surprised to hear they were offering Alexis a place on the team. Initially, I wondered if there'd been a mix-up, but it seemed Alexis had made an impression that warranted an opportunity.

When I relayed this news to Alexis, she burst into tears. She knew exactly how she had performed that day. There was no sugarcoating it. Because of that performance, she believed there was no way she could be good enough to join Premier. But, she agreed to try. So together, we focused on the process, not the outcome, paying attention only to daily improvements.

Over the next three months, I watched in awe as Alexis embraced the growth mindset and transformed into a strong and competent player. No, she wasn't scoring all the points or starting every game, but she was evolving in ways that surpass the confines of the basketball court. She stands taller, speaks more confidently, and has fostered better relationships with her teammates. Despite her initial instinct to retreat into a fixed mindset, believing she wasn't good enough, Alexis chose to trust in her ability to grow. She stepped out of her comfort zone, and the changes that have unfolded over the past few months have been nothing short of remarkable.

I've had a similar experience with my son, Jack, but on a different level. He's got loads of talent and is a confident nine-year- old. He is like a honey badger; he is fearless, and he is hyper aware that confidence is key to his success. With Jack, I have to change the scoreboard. In addition to asking, "Are we better than we were yesterday?" and talking about continuous growth, we focus on bravery, courage, hard work, and effort.

So, when he has a good football game and scores several touchdowns, I don't shower him with praise as he walks off the field. Many well-meaning parents would compliment talent, genius, and god given ability, in hopes of building his self esteem. But instead, I say, "Jack, that was an excellent performance. What did you do differently this week that allowed you to play at such a high level?" My aim is to direct his attention to the *work* that went into his achievement— the strenuous practice sessions, the mental preparation, and the continuous refinement of his skills. Because then he starts attributing his success to his hard work, and not solely his talent.

The time will come when Jack walks into a room where everyone is just as talented as he is, and I don't want him to feel intimidated or threatened. I want him to know that he can adapt, evolve, and compete at the highest level. Not because of some inborn talent, but because of his willingness to learn and to persevere.

The concept of growth versus fixed mindset isn't about becoming solely one or the other. Instead, it's about recognizing that we have both mindsets in different areas of our lives. The real question is: what's our plan to improve those areas where we lean more towards a fixed mindset?

Nunc Coepi

I had the pleasure of coaching and being around Phillip Rivers at North Carolina State University, and to be honest, he is one of the finest human beings I know. He consistently refers to the latin phrase "Nunc coepi" which translates to "Now, I begin." He used this mantra to remind him of the importance of constant growth and continually pressing that reset button to make the most of every moment.

Rivers has this unique blend of confidence and self-deprecation that is refreshingly authentic. He embodies the spirit of "Nunc coepi." To him, every day is a fresh start, an opportunity to begin again, to strive to be brave, to be courageous, and to put in the hard work. As he'd often say, "Today is the best day of the week and a great day to get better." His personality was contagious. In every sense of the word, he was a Tigger, a climber. He wasn't one to sit around idly; he was always striving to see just how far and how high he could go. To this day, I've yet to meet anyone quite like him.

While you may see many professional athletes tossing around inspirational phrases on TV, with Rivers, it was always genuine. He isn't your typical quarterback. He may not have the prettiest throw, he's not the fastest runner, and he's not the most graceful athlete. But he has had a long career full of successes, thanks to his growth mindset and his refusal to view any challenge as insurmountable. Rivers played seventeen years in the NFL, an achievement that stands as a testament to his remarkable mindset.

Because he focuses on the phrase "Nunc coepi," Rivers embodies the principles of resilience and continuous improvement. He understands that success is not solely determined by natural talent or physical abilities, but rather by one's mindset and determination to grow. By embracing the idea of "Now, I begin," Rivers approaches each day with a fresh perspective and a commitment to start anew, regardless of past achievements or setbacks.

This mindset has enabled Rivers to overcome obstacles and push beyond perceived limitations. He recognizes that every moment presents an opportunity for growth and uses this belief to motivate himself and inspire those around him. His genuine passion for improvement and his relentless work ethic have earned him the respect and admiration of teammates, coaches, and fans alike. And Rivers's success serves as a reminder that true greatness is not solely measured by physical attributes or natural talent, but rather by the unwavering commitment to self-improvement and the willingness to embrace challenges head-on.

Watch the Details

Too often, when we are young, we try to move too quickly. We skip steps, bypass the process, and hope we will still find success faster than anyone else. But, we only hurt ourselves when we do this. Skipping steps or blowing past them completely might get us there faster, but we will likely have to redo our work at some point and might even lose a good reputation. In the end, if you are trying to cheat anything, you're only really cheating yourself. Details matter.

When I was a child, my family and I would mow the lawn every Saturday. We weren't a particularly affluent family, but I remember taking immense pride in the appearance of our lawn. We would put in the work and then sit back, sip our homemade lemonade, and admire our handiwork. It was a small thing, but it mattered to us. The work to make our yard beautiful was always a team effort. We focused on detail.

When my brother KC worked for Michelin tires, Herm Edwards came to speak to his group. Herm is a former NFL player, Hall of Famer, Former Jets, Chiefs, and Arizona State Head coach. In his speech, he talked about the importance of putting your signature on things.

Many important things in our lives require our signature. Marriage license, mortgages, car loans, and even birth certificates. Other important times for signatures include our constitution, our declaration of independence and various other important legal documents. For those of you who have put your signature on a birth certificate of a child who struggled to arrive here on Earth, you know how it feels to sign that document. It's important. For the most part, your signature on a document signifies two things: ownership and/or accountability.

But, I would argue, our most important signatures are the ones that no one sees—the invisible, everyday details we take seriously. Will we complete this workout? Will we skip any repetitions? Will we put our best effort into this team? Will we prepare for this job interview? Our success is intimately tied to our willingness to "put our signature" on these small but crucial moments of our life. Our yard may have been visible to the rest of the world, but it was our willingness to focus on the details of the work that made it unique. Your success and your performance is tied to your willingness to put your signature on these small moments of your life.

Being attentive to the details is a key characteristic of a person with a growth mindset. They don't fear looking bad or making mistakes; instead, they're focused on self-improvement. People with a growth mindset understand the importance of doing things right, even if it takes a little longer. They take pride in their work. A growth mindset isn't just about striving to be better, it's also about respecting the process and knowing that the details are what make the difference in the long run.

Unraveling the Genius Paradox

According to Friedrich Nietzsche, "Our vanity, our self-love, promotes the cult of the genius. For if we think of genius as something magical, we are not obliged to compare ourselves and find ourselves lacking... To call someone 'divine' means: 'here there is no need to compete.'"[1] The idea of "genius" often holds us back from our potential. We see others who are amazing and think, "They are a genius. I just don't have their talent." But this is simply not true.

A few years ago, I had the privilege of attending a speech that struck a chord within me. The speaker, my friend Damian Dayton, is incredibly talented, funny, and authentic in his approach. He began by introducing himself as "Damian Dayton, 80% genius." He went on to list all his impressive accomplishments: ace soccer player, filmmaker, entrepreneur, product developer, and Chief Creative Officer for Creatably.com. On top of that, the guy's got a knack for creating hilarious videos that sell like hotcakes online. It's clear he's not your everyday Joe.

But what really makes Damian's speech unforgettable isn't just his impressive resume. It's the unexpected approach he takes. As he dove into the heart of his speech, he said, "Michael Jordan IS AN IDIOT. But also, he's a genius." Everyone in the room was practically holding their breath, waiting to see where he's going with this. Now, he's not denying Michael Jordan's basketball brilliance. But Damian also points out that Jordan was far from a perfect teammate—maybe even one of the worst. And then, in big, bold letters, he proclaims, "PHIL JACKSON WAS A GENIUS."

You see, Phil Jackson was the guy who understood what Michael Jordan, Dennis Rodman, and Scottie Pippen needed. He got that Jordan needed guidance, Rodman needed freedom, and Pippen deserved recognition. Under his wing, these athletes flourished. Jordan became the "G.O.A.T.", Rodman became the NBA's rebound king, and Pippen, well, he became one of the best second men in NBA history.

Then Damian shifts gears and goes, "ALBERT EINSTEIN WAS

A GENIUS. But he, too, was an idiot." Whoa, right? He tells us that Einstein, for all his brilliance in theoretical astrophysics, couldn't tie his shoelaces and nearly got expelled from elementary school. And then he asks: What if Einstein spent his life just trying to get better at tying his shoes? It would've been a waste of his true genius.

That's when Damian drops this bomb!

"There's a difference between being a genius and having genius. The former is static, but the latter, we can grow." He continues quietly, saying, "Everyone in this room is a genius."

Damian then went on to outline four fundamental steps to develop our own genius:

1. Ask people you trust, specifically those in your field or those close to you, "What do you think I am really good at?" This allows us to gain valuable insights and perspectives on our strengths.

2. Help others develop their genius. Be public in acknowledging their talents. By fostering an environment that supports growth, we contribute to the collective cultivation of genius.

3. Focus on your strengths and strive to become the best in the world at them. By harnessing and honing our greatest strengths, we create a foundation upon which our other abilities can flourish.

4. Ignore the haters. In the pursuit of our genius, detractors may emerge. Instead of allowing their negativity to deter us, we must remain steadfast and confident in our path.

We often look at incredible people—geniuses—and think, "I could never be like them." It's easy to get caught up in thinking that genius is this elusive, untouchable thing. Like it's only reserved for a chosen few.

Well, here's the kicker: that's just our own vanity and self-love tricking us.

The potential for greatness is within your grasp, and it starts with getting to know yourself better, finding out what makes you tick, and discovering what you're really passionate about. And, of course, it involves rolling up our sleeves and getting down to some good, old-fashioned, hard work.

Treat Triumph and Disaster Equally

My junior college football coach was a giant of a man. Standing just over 6'3" tall and weighing around 300 lbs, he was an imposing figure with an NFL career that included stints with the Raiders and the Broncos. Of Polynesian descent, Coach Uperesa was the epitome of cool, calm, and collected. In the two years I played for him, I only saw him lose his temper three times, and each time, there was a warning: his eyes. Those eyes struck fear in me like nothing else.

I'll never forget one incident that seemed to come out of the blue. We were watching film, and a receiver caught the ball on a third down and five, to convert a first down. As the player got up, he faced the home crowd in the stadium and pounded his chest two or three times. The video was instantly paused. "What is that?" Coach Uperesa asked as he pointed to the player. A few of us laughed . . . until we saw his eyes. He wasn't laughing. He was angry. "What is that?" he repeated.

The room fell silent, and no one dared to speak. Coach Upersea continued, "This stuff pisses me off. You're going to pound your chest for doing what you are supposed to do? You're going to bring attention to yourself because you did what you were taught to do? This team never has been, isn't now, and never will be about you." He looked each of us in the eye and asked, "Are we clear?" Many of us were too stunned to answer until prompted with another angry, "Are we clear!?"

We all answered in unison, "Yes, Sir!"

I've thought about this day hundreds of times since that crisp fall afternoon. In that room, as a young sophomore, I realized for the first time that life was not about me. Sport and business is filled with false bravado, and we constantly see others pounding their chest to bring attention to themselves. And you know what's funny? Most of the time, it's for doing precisely what they were *supposed* to do.

That day, Coach Uperesa made sure I would never be that person.

He wanted me to play for something bigger than myself. He wanted me to play with vision and focus on the team. He didn't want me to be the best player on the team; he wanted me to be the best player *for* our team. There's a significant difference. Ego is the number one way to self-destruct on the biggest of all stages. If you play a sport for yourself, or if all your endeavors are for your own ego and pride, success will always be fleeting. And, it will almost always escape you.

Have you ever ready the poem, "If" by Rudyard Kipling?[2] I'd like you to read through it now:

> If you can keep your head when all about you
> Are losing theirs and blaming it on you,
> If you can trust yourself when all men doubt you,
> But make allowance for their doubting too;
> If you can wait and not be tired by waiting,
> Or being lied about, don't deal in lies,
> Or being hated, don't give way to hating,
> And yet don't look too good, nor talk too wise:
>
> If you can dream—and not make dreams your master;
> If you can think—and not make thoughts your aim;
> If you can meet with Triumph and Disaster
> And treat those two impostors just the same;
> If you can bear to hear the truth you've spoken
> Twisted by knaves to make a trap for fools,
> Or watch the things you gave your life to, broken,
> And stoop and build 'em up with worn-out tools:
>
> If you can make one heap of all your winnings
> And risk it on one turn of pitch-and-toss,
> And lose, and start again at your beginnings
> And never breathe a word about your loss;
> If you can force your heart and nerve and sinew
> To serve your turn long after they are gone,
> And so hold on when there is nothing in you

---

2   " by Rudyard Kipling

Except the Will which says to them: 'Hold on!'
If you can talk with crowds and keep your virtue,
Or walk with Kings—nor lose the common touch,
If neither foes nor loving friends can hurt you,
If all men count with you, but none too much;
If you can fill the unforgiving minute
With sixty seconds' worth of distance run,
Yours is the Earth and everything that's in it,
And—which is more—you'll be a Man, my son!

Kipling's poem advises us how to steer through trials and triumphs. He says, "If you can meet triumph and disaster, and treat those two imposters just the same." This is a favorite line of mine because both triumph and disaster are fleeting. We cannot let either consume us.

Staying focused isn't just about not dwelling on losses. It's equally crucial not to get too swept up in our victories. Constantly brooding over our failures can derail our success. Basking in a win can distract us. If you scored a touchdown in the first quarter of a game, you wouldn't let your guard down for the rest of the game! Triumph or disaster, joy or disappointment—they're two sides of the same coin. Kipling's point is that life is a series of peaks and valleys. Whether we find ourselves standing on the mountaintop or in the depth of a valley, our attitude should remain unchanged.

Don't get me wrong, I'm not suggesting you should never indulge in the thrill of victory or allow yourself a moment of grief when you face a loss. But what I am saying is don't linger. Take five seconds, five minutes, or five days or so to fully experience these emotions, then get back to the task at hand. By doing this, you allow yourself to fully experience your feelings—be it elation or despair—before shifting your focus back to what truly counts: hard work and effort. Believe me, most of us probably hang on to both these states a little longer than we should. The trick is to acknowledge the feelings, give yourself a time limit, then get back to work.

CHALLENGE 1

Put your name on everything you do today. Make yourself proud of your effort. Notice that I said effort. There is no such thing as perfection in this life. However, the pursuit of perfection allows us to feel complete and whole. It allows us to progress and improve. So work on the details today, stay present in the moment, and take note of how much your focus increases.

CHALLENGE 2

Throughout your day, notice moments of triumph and disaster, no matter how small. These could range from completing a difficult task, to making a mistake, or even missing a bus. Reflect on how you react to these moments. Are you over celebrating your wins or wallowing in your losses? After identifying these moments, set a timer for five minutes. Allow yourself this time to fully experience the emotion—be it elation from a victory or disappointment from a loss. Once the timer ends, consciously redirect your focus back to your next task. Your goal is not to suppress your emotions, but rather to give them their due time without letting them distract you from your ongoing work.

CONCLUSION

Before we finish, I want you to think about that last time you were truly brave. What did that look like? Was it a declaration of love? A bold statement of your beliefs? A stand for your people or your culture? Or was it as simple—and as monumental—as speaking your mind?

Think about the courage you've shown in the workplace, on the field, or on the court. Remember the time you took the last second shot, the time you stepped up to handle a challenging task, or that moment when you voiced an innovative idea. All of these are moments of bravery.

I hope these moments are recent and that with the help of this book, bravery can become your second nature. A couple of years ago, I watched two young quarterbacks, just 18-years-old, going toe-to-toe in the national championship game. Despite the inevitable mistakes, the interceptions, and the fumbles, they displayed remarkable courage. They weren't frightened of the big stage, and they played their hearts out. Remember their fearlessness as you exercise your own bravery this week. Go ahead and speak your mind—just do it kindly, without undue emotion. Take a chance, give someone a call, compliment a colleague, start a podcast, ask someone to dinner, or start that hobby you've been thinking about for years. It's never too late to become the person you were meant to be.

The biggest thing I want you to walk away with is the goal to be courageous at least one minute a day. Pure unadulterated guts, even if it is only for sixty seconds today, will change your confidence, motivation, and outlook on life. Everything I've talked about in this book takes guts. When things get hard, these tactics are not always easy to remember. But, they are the keys to some of the biggest successes I have witnessed.

Perhaps you've noticed that I didn't devote a whole section to overcoming fear and anxiety. Instead, I've sprinkled anti-fear, anti-anxiety tools throughout the book. Confidence, as we've learned, is the best antidote to these emotions. Deliberate practice, imagery, visualization—these are all means to grow your confidence, to become fearless, and to embrace opportunities with open arms. Because the goal is to become a lion.

The lion doesn't fret over not being the fastest or the largest animal in the jungle. It embraces its own strengths, its own unique capabilities. The lion's success doesn't stem from being the best; it comes from courage, an unshakable faith in its abilities, and a willingness to seize every opportunity. This is the mindset I invite you to adopt. Be bold, be courageous, be a lion. Step into each new day with conviction and strength, unafraid to take chances and to seize opportunities.

Before I close, I want to express my deep gratitude to you for coming on this journey with me. I love your guts. I hope this book has been as transformative for you as writing it has been for me. So, thank you for reading, for choosing courage, and for stepping into the arena. Keep showing up. Keep being brave. And remember to roar!

ADDITIONAL RESOURCES

Mindset Matters Podcast

Fuel your journey to greatness with the Mindset Matters podcast by Riley Jensen on iTunes. This is more than just a podcast—it's your daily dose of inspiration and motivation, perfectly designed to uplift you during your commute or prime your mindset before a competition. As your host I dive into a world of insights to help you awaken the champion within. Tune in at: Mindset Matters Podcast.

RJ Performance Group

Get in touch with me at *www.rjpg.net* where I can provide expert coaching and tailored programs to meet your needs. Remember, those who reach the top—whether in sports or business—know that you must first master your mind before you can master your performance.

At RJ Performance, we work closely with our clients to develop in key areas such as:

- Awareness
- Goal-setting
- Relaxation Techniques
- Confidence Building
- Resiliency Training
- Dealing with Pressure
- Imagery

- Focus & Concentration
- Pre-Performance Preparation
- Decision Making
- Injury Mental Training

We're committed to helping parents, coaches, and individuals uncover the best practices for developing mental toughness. Our programs are science-based and experience-driven, specifically designed to address your unique situation and goals.

Mental Toughness Sessions

Our Mental Toughness Sessions are individual sessions with our sport psychology practitioners are designed to bring about immediate impact and sustainable improvement in your performance:

- Discover your character strengths, your "why," and develop a personal philosophy.
- Focus on control—learn to ignore what you can't control and concentrate on what you can.
- Enhance your focus and concentration to maximize your potential.
- Use the power of imagery, a proven tool for enhancing performance.
- Master positive Self-Talk—reduce negative thoughts and focus on empowering narratives.
- Develop effective Pre-Performance Routines to lower your sport-anxiety and improve performance.

Check out our website at www.rjpg.net to see the next mental toughness camp available.

Book Me for a Speaking Event

Looking for an impactful speaker for your company, team, or sporting event? I'm available! I commonly speak on courage, mental toughness, motivation, and more. As a coach and speaker, my goal is to unlock your potential, whether you're an individual, a team, a business, or a parent of an aspiring athlete. I would love to come and help motivate!

You can book me for a speaking event www.rjpg.net

Or you can book me for a corporate training www.rjpg.net

ACKNOWLEDGEMENTS

Sport has always been a significant part of my life. I am thankful for the incredible coaches, teammates, mentors, friends, and family I've had by my side.

A significant mention goes to my biggest supporter and best teammate, my wife Georgann. She's been there for me supporting outlandish ideas with a unique touch and significant grace. I've pushed the limits more times than I can imagine, but she has always been a driving force. Thank you, G, for always being patient and understanding with me. It still amazes me how you've supported all of my truly sustainable dreams. The life and family we have built mean everything to me, and I am grateful for the strong foundation you've set for my children and me.

To my children Alexis, Jack, and Karissa, I genuinely hope this book makes a difference in your lives much like these concepts have influenced mine. You three are my daily reminder that this world is full of endless possibility.

And finally, I couldn't have written this book without an amazing team around me. A sincere thank you to all of my friends who've always been supportive, especially those who kept pushing me along with the question, "When are you writing your book?" I especially want to thank my Mother Troy Jensen, my Father Kirk Jensen, Quinn Wheeler, Andrew Taylor, Jen Barlow, and George Manolis. Your feedback, encouragement, and belief in me have made all the difference. I love your guts. Here's to good things to come!

ABOUT THE AUTHOR

Riley Jensen brings a wealth of experience and expertise to the realm of mental performance coaching. He has been the lead Mental Performance Coach for Real Salt Lake and the Real Monarchs, and he is currently the lead Mental Performance Coach for Utah State University Athletics and Weber State University Athletics. In addition, Riley works with USA Archery (Para), Westminster College Basketball, and individual athletes ranging from the Olympic, World Cup, professional, collegiate, to high school levels. His professional reach extends into the corporate world too, working with companies such as the Utah revenue department, LGCY Power sales associates and leadership, BSN Sports, Boston Scientific, Abbot, Interior Worx, Michelin, Wise Company, Fusion Imaging, Hankook Tires, and Clyde Companies. Riley earned his B.A. from Utah State University and completed his M.S. in Sport and Performance Psychology at the University of Utah, where he also interned with the University's football and tennis teams.

Riley's passion and skill in teaching concepts like resilience, confidence, positivity, grit, and personal mastery set him apart in his field. His services are available to athletes across all levels and sports, as well as coaches, organizations, and businesses. From the locker room to the boardroom, Riley is a sought-after motivational speaker, helping individuals, teams, and businesses unlock their maximum potential.

With a football career spanning over 30 years, Riley has played and coached at high school and collegiate levels. He's also the co-founder and part owner of the Mountain West Elite sports camps that operate in several states. As a player, Riley started as a quarterback at an NCAA D1 school (USU), and was named 1st team junior college All-American QB at Snow College, where he was inducted into the Snow College Football Hall of Fame in 2017. His coaching experience extends to a Division 1 program (NC State) and several successful high school teams in the Salt Lake City area (Cottonwood, Olympus, Alta).

Outside of his professional commitments, Riley enjoys living life to the fullest in Salt Lake City, Utah. He loves spending quality time with his wife Georgann, and their three children. He loves to coach his children in sport as well. Through his work, his family, and his passions, Riley Jensen continues to inspire and influence those around him, promoting a mindset of success and resilience.

BIBLIOGRAPHY

Benjamin, D. J., Kimball, M. S., Heffetz, O., & Rees-Jones, A. (2012). What Do You Think Would Make You Happier? What Do You Think You Would Choose?*. *The American economic review.*

Brown, B. (2022). Listening to Shame.

Churchill, W. (n.d.). From https://www.nationalchurchillmuseum.org/never-give-in-never-never-never.html

Churchill, W. (n.d.). From https://www.goodreads.com/quotes/407062-you-will-never-reach-your-destination-if-you-stop-and

Clear, J. (2018). *Atomic Habits.*

Coyle, D. (2009). *The Talent Code.*

Davenport, B. (2022, October 1). From htatps://liveboldandbloom.com/10/self-confidence/self-confidence-quotes

Duckworth, A. (2018). *Grit.*

Duckworth, H. (2016). *Grit: The Power of Passion and Perseverance.*

Edison, T. (n.d.). From https://www.inspairingquotes.us/quotes/tROF_1CUnBowH

Eliot, G. (n.d.). From https://quoteinvestigator.com/2013/11/24/never-too-late/#:~:text=Dear%20Quote%20Investigator%3A%20My%20favorite%20quotation%20about%20untapped,on%20refrigerator%20magnets%2C%20posters%2C%20shirts%2C%20and%20key%20chains.

Gucciardi, Hanton, & Mallett. (2012). Grit, Mental Toughness, and Hardiness at the Elite Athlete Level. *Journal of Physical Education and Sport.*

Hamilton, L. (2023). From www.surfertoday.com

Harris, R. (2016). *The Happiness Trap.*

Kinderman, P., Schwannauer, M., Pontin, E., & Tai, S. (2013). Psychological Processes Mediate the Impact of Familial Risk, Social Circumstances, and Life Events on Mental Health. *PLoS ONE.*

Kipling, R. (1943). From https://www.poetry.com/poem/33247/if.

Kraus, M., Huang, C., & Keltner, D. (2010). Tactile communication, cooperation, and performance: an ethological study of the NBA. *Emotion.*

Lantz, Michel, & Glickman. (2018). The Role of Grit in Predicting Athletic Success and Mental Toughness in NCAA Division I Athletes.

Monson, T. S. (2013). I Will Not Fail Thee, nor Forsake Thee.

Morin, A. (2015). 7 Scientifically Proven Benefits of Gratitude. *Psychology Today.*

Morin, A. (2015). 7 Scientifically Proven Benefits of Gratitude. *Psychology Today.*

Mormon, B. o. (1830). *The Book of Mormon.*

Nietzsche, F. (n.d.). From https://www.bing.com/search?q=nietzsche+our+va nity+quote+our+self0love&qs=n&form=QBRE&sp=-1&ghc=1&lq=0&p q=nietzsche+our+vanity+quote+our+self0love&sc=4-40&sk=&cvid=6F-02B455E90E4D1FB89FB1FACDAD8243&ghsh=0&ghacc=0&ghpl=

Richter, C. (1958).

Roosevelt, T. (1910). The Man in the Arena.

Sills, D. (2011). The No. 1 Contributor to Happiness. *Pschology Today.*

Summitt, P. (2023). From https://graciousquotes.com/pat-summitt/#:~:text=%E2%80%9C%20Winning%20is%20fun%E2%80%A6%20 Sure.%20But%20winning%20is,satisfied%20with%20what%20 you%E2%80%99ve%20done%20is%20the%20point.%E2%80%9D

Taylor, J. B. (2009). *My Stroke of Insight: A Brain Scientist's Personal Journey.*

Tod, D., Hardy, J., & Oliver, E. (2011). Effects of Self-Talk: A Systematic Review. *J Sport Exerc Psychol.*

Tolle, E. (2021). From https://hackspirit.com/20-profound-quotes-eckhart-tolle-will-help-let-go-ego-embrace-every-moment-life/

Twain, M. (n.d.). From https://www.goodreads.com/quotes/505050-the-two-most-important-days-in-your-life-are-the

Twain, M. (n.d.). From https://timeular.com/blog/eat-frog/

Vernacchia, R. (2003). *Inner strength: The mental dynamics of athletic performance.* . Palo Alto: Warde Publishers.

Walter, N., Nikoleizig, L., & Alfermann, D. (2019). Effects of Self-Talk Training on Competitive Anxiety, Self-Efficacy, Volitional Skills, and Performance: An Intervention Study with Junior Sub-Elite Athletes. *Sports (Basel).*

White, S. (2023). From https://www.positivityblog.com/badass-quotes/

Young, S. (n.d.). From https://www.azquotes.com/author/21679-Steve_Young

Printed in the USA
CPSIA information can be obtained
at www.ICGtesting.com
LVHW011645271223
767218LV00007B/266

9 781637 926321